Differentiating Instruction With Style

This book belongs to:

Name *Ms. Tanguay*

Other Corwin Press Books by Gayle H. Gregory

Differentiated Literacy Strategies for Student Growth and Achievement in Grades 7–12
by Gayle H. Gregory and Lin Kuzmich, 2005

Differentiated Literacy Strategies for Student Growth and Achievement in Grades K-6
by Gayle H. Gregory and Lin Kuzmich, 2005

Data Driven Differentiation in the Standards-Based Classroom
by Gayle H. Gregory and Lin Kuzmich, 2004

*Differentiated Instructional Strategies in Practice: Training, Implementation, and
    Supervision*
by Gayle H. Gregory, 2003

Differentiated Instructional Strategies: One Size Doesn't Fit All
by Gayle H. Gregory and Carolyn Chapman, 2002

Thinking Inside the Block Schedule: Strategies for Teaching in Extended Periods of Time
by Pam Robbins, Gayle H. Gregory, and Lynne E. Herndon, 2000

Differentiating Instruction With Style

Aligning Teacher and Learner Intelligences for
Maximum Achievement

Gayle H. Gregory

CORWIN PRESS
A SAGE Publications Company
Thousand Oaks, California

For information:

Corwin Press
A Sage Publications Company
2455 Teller Road
Thousand Oaks, California 91320
E-mail: order@corwinpress.com

Sage Publications Ltd.
1 Oliver's Yard
55 City Road
London EC1Y 1SP
United Kingdom

Sage Publications India Pvt. Ltd.
B-42, Panchsheel Enclave
Post Box 4109
New Delhi 110 017 India

Printed in the United States of America.

Library of Congress Cataloging-in-Publication Data

Gregory, Gayle.
Differentiating instruction with style: aligning teacher and learner intelligences for maximum achievement / Gayle H. Gregory.
    p. cm.
Includes bibliographical references and index.
ISBN 0-7619-3161-9 (cloth) — ISBN 0-7619-3162-7 (pbk.)
  1. Individualized instruction. 2. Cognitive styles in children.
3. Mixed ability grouping in education. I. Title.
LB1031.G744 2005
371.39′4—dc22

                       2005003286

This book is printed on acid-free paper.

05   06   07   08   09   10   9 8 7 6 5 4 3 2 1

Acquisitions Editor:	Faye Zucker
Editorial Assistant:	Gem Rabanera
Production Editor:	Tracy Alpern
Copy Editor:	Linda Gray
Proofreader:	Christine Dahlin
Typesetter:	C&M Digitals (P) Ltd.
Indexer:	Gloria Tierney
Cover Designer:	Anthony Paular
Graphic Designer:	Lisa Miller

Contents

Brain research and educational research tell us that people learn in many different ways and styles. This chapter provides a brief overview of the scope of available theories of intelligences and thinking styles. You don't need to know every detail of every theory, but you can use an understanding of learning styles theory to explore the diversity that each learner brings to the classroom.

The natural process of learning involves emotional, social, physical, cognitive, and reflective learning systems. Teachers can use an understanding of these learning systems, of common brain principles, and of how the left and right brain hemispheres interact to create safe, friendly, and challenging classrooms; to plan brain-compatible lessons; and to select teaching strategies that engage both hemispheres of the brain.

Understanding how people prefer to learn involves surveying them, listening to them, observing them, and understanding how their preferences for visual, auditory, or kinesthetic modes affect their learning. Important theories about learning preferences and learning styles have been offered to us by researchers in psychology and education, including Carl Jung, Anthony Gregorc, David Kolb, Bernice McCarthy, Don Lowry, Richard Strong, Harvey Silver, and J. R. Hanson. To synthesize their many theories into four primary learning styles, we will meet beach ball learners, puppy learners, microscope learners, and clipboard learners, introducing principles for differentiated lesson planning and instruction that work for all.

Preface

It has been a journey of discovery as I have explored the art and craft of teaching. When I started out years ago, I didn't have any idea that I would be still trying to "figure" things out today.

As a young woman in the 1960s my career choices were secretarial work, cosmetology, nursing, or teaching. My father recommended teaching as a great career for me because I could get a job anywhere my husband was transferred and I would have the summers off to be with my children. There were limited options for women then, and originally I did think that I would stop teaching when I had a family. Well, this exciting journey has lasted much longer than I expected.

Part of that journey for me has been the move from the "one size fits all" model of instruction to recognizing that our schools and classrooms are full of diverse learners who have different backgrounds from "nature and nurture." Instrumental in knowing our learners is being knowledgeable about their different learning styles and the different ways we all have of being intelligent. Teachers who have the tools, repertoire, and "style" to respond to their learners' differences will be able to intrigue, engage, and teach them everyday in ways that ensure their continuing growth and achievement. This book can help you explore the diversity of styles, intelligences, and thinking in your classroom so that all students may reach their potential.

Acknowledgments

I have been enlightened and influenced by great thinkers, including Howard Gardner, Robert Sternberg, Daniel Goleman, Art Costa, Bob Garmstom, Pat Wolfe, Robert Sylwester, Barbara Givens, David Sousa, Tony Gregorc, Carol Rolheiser, Bob Marzano, Jay McTighe, Carol Ann Tomlinson, Pam Robbins, Heidi Hayes Jacob, Grant Wiggins, Richard Stiggins, Doug Reeves, Linda Elder, and Richard Paul.

As always, I thank my husband Joe and my family for their patience and understanding of the time this venture took from "family hour." I could not accomplish anything worthwhile without their love and support.

It is my hope and desire that this book will be a helpful, insightful addition to the libraries of teachers, administrators, and other educators and an integral part of their planning and thinking as they design learning for all children so that all may learn and reach their potential.

—*Gayle H. Gregory*

Corwin Press and the author extend their thanks to the following reviewers for their contributions to this volume:

Nancy Creech, Dort Elementary School, Roseville, MI

William Fitzhugh, Reisterstown Elementary School, Reisterstown, MD

Steve Hutton, Elementary School Principal, Villa Hills, KY

About the Author

 **Gayle H. Gregory** has been a teacher in elementary, middle, and secondary schools. For many years, she taught in schools with extended periods of instructional time (block schedules). She has had extensive districtwide experience as a curriculum consultant and staff development coordinator. She was course director at York University for the Faculty of Education, teaching in the teacher education program. She now consults internationally (Europe, Asia, North and South America, Australia) with teachers, administrators, and staff developers in the areas of managing change, differentiated instruction, brain-compatible learning, block scheduling, emotional intelligence, instructional and assessment practices, cooperative group learning, presentation skills, renewal of secondary schools, enhancing teacher quality, and coaching and mentoring.

Gayle is affiliated with many organizations, including the Association for Supervision and Curriculum Development and the National Staff Development Council. She is the author of *Differentiated Instructional Strategies in Practice: Training, Implementation, and Supervision* and the coauthor of *Designing Brain-Compatible Learning; Thinking Inside the Block Schedule: Strategies for Teaching in Extended Periods of Time; Differentiated Instructional Strategies: One Size Doesn't Fit All; Data Driven Differentiation in the Standards-Based Classroom; Differentiated Literacy Strategies for Student Growth and Achievement in Grades K-6;* and *Differentiated Literacy Strategies for Student Growth and Achievement in Grades 7–12.* She has been featured in Video Journal of Education's bestselling elementary and secondary videos *Differentiating Instruction to Meet the Needs of All Learners.*

Gayle is committed to lifelong learning and professional growth for herself and others. She may be contacted by e-mail at gregorygayle@netscape .net. Her Web site is www3.sympatico.ca/gayle.gregory.

Introduction

DIFFERENTIATING INSTRUCTION WITH STYLE

Like many other educators of my vintage, I have seen many things come and go—mandates and policies, theories and innovations that were "flavor of the month" one semester and replaced the next. The last 20 years have been an accelerated learning curve for most educators, filled with information about the brain, research on instructional strategies, intentional planning with standards or outcomes and schoolwide collaboration that focuses on student learning and problem solving. We are beginning to move from the "one size fits all" model to recognizing that our schools and classrooms are full of diverse learners who have different backgrounds from "nature and nurture."

Thus it is so important for teachers to get to know those learners, tap into their strengths, and respond with differentiated activities and experiences that will intrigue and engage them. But to differentiate instruction, we first have to know the learners. Instrumental in knowing the learners is becoming knowledgeable about learning styles, the different ways we have of being intelligent, and the tools and repertoire appropriate for responding to those differences.

Brain Research

In this book, the brain's natural learning system will be explored. The principles of how the brain operates and the basic functions will be explained to set a context for learning. The interaction of the right and left hemispheres of the brain—*hemisphericity*—is integral to the learning process. This book examines the functions of each hemisphere as well as how to engage the whole brain in the learning process.

Learning Styles

Although we have discussed learning styles and multiple intelligences in the other books on *Differentiated Instructional Strategies* (Gregory & Chapman, 2002; Gregory, 2003; Gregory & Kuzmich, 2004; Gregory &

Kuzmich, 2005a, 2005b), we have given them limited attention as part of a more comprehensive approach to differentiation. This book will focus in more depth on the variety of learning styles frameworks and theories available for consideration and use by teachers.

Which learning styles theories and frameworks teachers choose from and among is less important than teachers' decisions to use learning styles as a way to get to know their students better and tap into the different preferences learners have through intentional planning. This book will provide an overview of the most popular and well-known learning styles and then offer suggestions for using that information in planning. It is also helpful for students to know about the diversity of preferences, styles, and dispositions in themselves and others to better understand and respond to the differences in their peers.

Intelligences

Intelligent Behaviors (Habits of Mind)

Art Costa's (Costa, 1991; Costa & Garmston, 1994, 2002) intelligent behaviors will be discussed. These behaviors can be developed in students so that they become more intelligent in their ways of learning and living.

Multiple Intelligences

We have learned and accepted over the years that there are many ways to be smart. Howard Gardner introduced us to seven intelligences and added an eighth later on. This theory, used naturally in planning thematic instruction by early elementary teachers, has been supported through research and study using criteria to substantiate all eight of the intelligences.

Gardner admits he is surprised by the reaction of teachers and the vast variety of ways they have found to use the theory in the classroom. We will revisit Gardner's eight multiple intelligences in this book, and you will find planning frameworks that consider both the intelligences and the learning styles as well. Several inventories for students are also included.

Successful Intelligence

Robert Sternberg's (1996) successful intelligence includes our ability to use information and knowledge practically, analytically, and creatively rather than just knowing facts and figures.

Emotional Intelligence

Daniel Goleman's (1995, 1998) emotional intelligences include five domains from which one needs to have skills and abilities to be competent and capable members of society. These skills and how to promote them and integrate them into the curriculum will be discussed.

Thinking Styles

Students need to develop skills in both creative and critical thinking. Thinking is important to include in the curriculum as well as the types and styles of thinking. The taxonomies and tools I will discuss include the following:

- Bloom (1956)
- Quellmalz (1985)
- Krathwohl's affective taxonomy (Krathwohl, Bloom, & Masia, 1964)
- Graphic organizers
- SCAMPER (Eberle, 1982)
- Williams's creative taxonomy (Williams, 1989)

You Don't Need to Differentiate Every Detail

Differentiating for the diversity of learning styles, intelligences, and thinking in your classroom does not mean that you have to know every detail of every theory and individualize for every student. Simply becoming conscious of the collective needs of students is a way to get to know them better, tap into their preferences through intentional planning, explore the diversity that they bring to the classroom, and make the right choices for your classroom.

Learning, Growth, and the Brain

1

In recent years, what we have learned about how the brain is organized and functions raises questions for us as teachers. According to Ornstein (1986), the brain is a complex biological organ made of several systems embedded within its structures:

> Stuck side by side, inside the skin, inside the skull, are several special purpose, separate, and specific small minds. The particular collection of talents, abilities, and capacities that each person possesses depends partly on birth and partly on experience. Our illusion is that each of us is somehow unified with a single coherent purpose and action . . . [but] we are not a single person. We are many. . . . All of these general components of the mind can act independently of each other, [and] they may well have different priorities. (pp. 8–9)

These functions are not processed consciously but occur automatically. The truth is that the brain naturally learns what it needs to if there is useful information, if the information is interesting, and if the challenge is appropriate.

THE NATURAL PROCESS OF LEARNING

Restak (1994) identifies five systems that are constantly interacting, with multiple connections, as we accept, process, and interpret information. This is like a 24/7 "multiplex theater" according to Barbara Given (2002), where multiple movies are showing simultaneously. The five systems are the emotional learning system, the social learning system, the physical learning system, the cognitive learning system, and the reflective learning system.

Emotional Learning System

Emotions and social interactions that affect feelings can inhibit academic progress (Rozman, 1998). For example, students will seek first to be safe and comfortable before they care what there is to be learned. Emotional nourishment is essential from birth to death (Kessler, 2000; Palmer, 1993), and emotions have a huge effect on the ability to focus and learn. Endorphins and norepinephrine (the feel-good neurotransmitters released in the brain during positive experiences) contribute to learning as well as to good health (Pert, 1993). Emotions are both innate and acquired, learned from peers and parents throughout life but especially in the early years (Harris, 1998).

When our emotional needs are met, the brain produces serotonin (a feel-good neurotransmitter). Sometimes young people turn to drugs to eradicate the negative feelings in their lives, but feeling good without drugs can occur when students feel included and part of the group—that "warm, feel-good" reaction when they know someone cares. Csikszentmihalyi (1990) refers to the "state of flow" where attention is focused and one's skill level is matched with an appropriate challenge. In this state, a person feels "in the groove" and capable and empowered to be successful.

The emotional system is embellished in classrooms and schools with the following attributes:

- Where educators and students believe all students will learn
- Where students' differences are honored
- Where teachers connect the learning to students' lives
- Where teachers provide multiple ways for students to show what they know
- Where teachers continue to challenge students appropriately at their level
- Where the climate is supportive, inclusive, and predictable
- Where students and teachers celebrate the gains toward targeted standards
- Where students and teachers can laugh and celebrate together
- Where intrinsic motivation and pride in a "job well done" is fostered
- Where students' intrinsic motivation is cultivated through goal setting and reflection

Social Learning System

Part of the developmental process through the first few years of life is to form relationships with others. A system in place at birth relates to paired relationships. Another system progresses toward group relationships (Harris, 1998). It is a basic human need to feel that we belong and are accepted and included. Feelings of comfort, trust, respect, and affection increase the brain's feel-good neurotransmitter levels (Panksepp, 1998). Often in classrooms there is such a quest to "cover the standards" that there is no opportunity to develop social interactions that promote trust and connections even though we know students will learn better in a supportive environment. A kinship fostered by group norms and values is more conducive to learning (Wright, 1994). Robert Sapolsky in his book *Why Zebras Don't Get Ulcers* suggests that social support has a huge impact on student learning. Students who feel part of the group and accepted by their peers are more confident and experience less stress in difficult learning situations. It is essential that teachers create a community of learners where every student feels a sense of belonging. A teacher who is aware of this need can capitalize on this knowledge by creating a classroom climate that provides the following:

- Respect for all learners
- Recognition for students' hopes and aspirations
- A multisensory environment for real-world learning (Given, 2002)

The use of cooperative group learning is essential in a classroom, not only to allow the social system to flourish but also to help students achieve academic goals as well as social skills.

Physical Learning System

The physical learning system has to do with active involvement in learning. In classrooms, this is often the system that is not used enough even though we know that gifted students (Milgram, Dunn, & Price, 1993) and underachievers (R. Dunn, 1990) will benefit from active, tactile, and kinesthetic involvement with new material.

If we ignore this system, the learners will find a way to "actively" satisfy their needs in spite of our plans. The movement might seem a disruption and have nothing to do with the lesson at hand. So how do we build in opportunities for hands-on, active learning, or do we let students find their own ways, which may be counterproductive to learning? The physical system also demands movement to lower stress (adrenalin and cortisol, stress hormones in the blood stream) and supply more oxygen and glucose to the brain. Paul and Gail Dennison's book *Brain Gym* offers suggestions and activities to "wake up the brain" and integrate the right and left hemispheres.

Cognitive Learning System

The cognitive system deals with learning and focuses on consciousness, language development, attention, and memory. The senses are engaged in actively processing information. Facilitating learning by providing information in a novel way—one that stimulates all senses, including the visual, auditory, and tactile senses as well as taste and smell if appropriate—is something good teachers do.

The emotional, social, and physical systems seem greedy for attention, and if their needs are not met, students will not be able to focus on learning; thus the cognitive system cannot work optimally. If all systems' needs are met, students tend to be more attentive and engaged in the learning process and ultimately are more successful in their learning.

Reflective Learning System

It has been said that people learn from experience only if they reflect on the experience. This intelligence includes "thinking strategies, positive attitudes toward investing oneself in good thinking, and metacognition—awareness and management of one's own mind" (Perkins, 1995, p. 234). Damasio (1999) notes that the reflective system involves the interdependence of memory systems, communication systems, reason, attention, emotion, social awareness, physical experiences, and sensory modalities.

The reflective system allows us to do the following:

- Revisit and analyze situations
- Explore and react with ideas
- Create plans
- Facilitate progress toward goals

With limited time and multiple standards to achieve, this may be the system that is ignored in the classroom. These skills of continuous reflection and self-awareness are key to growth. The skills of metacognition and reflection enable students to form a complete image of self and to develop the strategies necessary to self-directed learning and success in life.

Figure 1.1 lists needs and preferences within each system and suggests classroom activities/strategies that teachers can use to satisfy those needs and preferences.

SAFETY AND THE SURVIVAL BRAIN

The brain was put in the head not to go to school but to survive on the savannah. Its first tasks toward survival are to get upright and mobile, communicate, and develop trust through interpersonal relationships.

Figure 1.1   The Five Natural Learning Systems in the Classroom

System	Needs and Preferences	Classroom Strategies
Emotional system Passion	• Positive climate • Emotional safety • Relevancy and meaning • Supportive learning community • Tapping into range of emotions Teacher as cheerleader, mentor	Build the classroom community and a positive climate by • Building trust • Providing appropriate challenge and feedback • Adjusting assignments
Social system Cooperation	• Inclusion • Respect • Enjoy others • Interaction • Interpersonal sharing • Authentic situations • Tolerance and diversity honored Teacher as consultant, coach	• Developing norms • Using teambuilding activities • Outlawing "put downs" • Using cooperative group learning • Simulations
Cognitive system Intention	• Promotes academic skill development • Connects prior learning and new learning • Seeks patterns, concepts, themes • Likes to see parts and the whole Teacher as facilitator	• Thinking skills • Graphic organizers • Advance organizers • Note taking and summarizing • Hypothesizing • Problem solving
Physical system Action	• Requires active involvement • Enjoys challenging tasks that encourage practice • Skills are a major part of this system Teacher as coach	• Mime • Pantomime • Role play • Building models • Hands on • Manipulatives • Simulations
Reflective system Introspective	• Personal reflection on one's own learning styles • Reflects on successes, failures, changes needed • Metacognition of one's strengths and preferences Teacher as gold miner	• Logs • Journals • Tickets out • Goal setting • PMI

Unfortunately, when we look around schools, many classrooms are diametrically opposite to these basic human quests. Classrooms where students are to stay in desks, not talk to others, and compete against their peers do not support the brain's natural functions and tendencies. This produces undue stress, and when there is stress, no thinking takes place. A person concerned with basic needs is not able to attend to the learning that should be taking place. The brain is no longer functioning in the neocortex but in the reptilian brain where there is no language or thought processing but instead a basic "fight or flight" reaction.

If students are controlled to the point where there is no option or choice to pursue learning in their own style or to show what they know in their own way, they will be stressed. If they have to find the one right answer by doing only one prescribed task, this may add unnecessary stress (and boredom) for the learner.

Choice and options give learners a sense of control over their own learning. The optimal climate we should be striving for is *high challenge, low threat,* where skill and task are balanced so that students can see success while stretching their skills and thinking. Csikszentmihalyi (1990) refers to this condition as flow, where the following conditions exist:

- Challenge and skill level are well matched.
- Choice and options are available.
- Feedback is ongoing.
- There is an intrinsic sense of satisfaction.
- Time goes by unnoticed.
- The learner is in the groove.
- Students are inspired by the task or activity to persevere.

This is a mammoth challenge when there is one teacher and a classroom full of diverse learners, but paying attention to learning styles and using strategies to give students choice and options give flow a greater chance of happening.

Not only is physical safety necessary in the classroom but so are emotional and psychological safety. Students need to know they are safe to share ideas and offer opinions without fear of ridicule, sarcasm, teasing, and antagonism from teachers or other students. This kind of positive climate is facilitated through the following:

- Norms that students generate and support (rules to live by)
- An orderly and consistent environment that is nurturing and patient
- Choice and options rather than control
- Respect for diversity: cultural, thinking, learning style
- Positive reinforcement and encouragement
- Invitational approaches that engage rather than exclude
- A sense of community and belonging in the group

BRAIN-COMPATIBLE LESSON PLANNING

Madeline Hunter (2004) was not far off what we now call brain-compatible learning. Her lesson-planning model looks at seven steps that teachers should consider in planning a lesson.

1. **Activating prior knowledge:** Opening mental files and setting the context of learning. Capturing attention. Providing an overview. Any information stored in long-term memory needs to be recalled and brought to short-term memory.

2. **Stating the objectives and purpose:** Tying the learning to the standards and/or outcomes to provide relevancy. The brain likes to know purpose and responds to meaningful and useful information.

3. **Instructional phase/input:** Providing information and content to develop concepts and skills. The Hunter model suggests that this is a didactic process; however, it can be done in a variety of ways: lecturette, video, jigsaw, guest speaker, text, or through the use of other technologies.

4. **Modeling:** Showing the learner what the skill looks like and sounds like. Providing a pattern for the brain to follow.

5. **Checking for understanding:** Students can show what they know or understand in a variety of ways, including writing, retelling, and demonstrating.

6. **Practice and application:** With the information, and after modeling by the teacher, students can apply their knowledge and skills in a practical way in situations that are meaningful and relevant to their own lives. Problem solving, projects, centers, and stations give ample opportunities for hands-on application and creativity. The brain loves novelty and relevance, and meaning is key to learning. These forms of application tap into all theaters of the mind.

7. **Closure and extension:** Bringing the lesson to closure is important to the brain because it doesn't like loose ends and wants to see the big picture. Opportunities for extension of the learning and challenging those learners who are at a higher level of readiness or ability may be offered.

SEVEN COMMON BRAIN PRINCIPLES

The following concepts have been gleaned from notable educators and researchers who have followed in Madeline Hunter's footsteps. These include Pat Wolfe (2001), David Sousa (2001), Barbara Given (2002), Robert Sylwester (2005), Renate and Geoffrey Caine (1991, 1997), and others.

1. Pattern Recognition and Schemas

The brain operates on probability based on past experiences. Schemas are patterns, clusters, arrangements, and categories stored together and understood. This is how we develop concepts by identifying like attributes of ideas. Chaining is the process of making connections by finding commonalities. Dr. Mel Levine (1990) calls this "horizontal threading." The brain checks its filing system to find other ideas and concepts that may be connected to the new learning. The brain will reject useless patterns and pieces of information that are not connected to what it already knows or finds intriguing.

Implications for Learning

Past experiences are unique and specific to each learner. Meaning comes from making connections, and without schemas, students' connections are not complete. Schemas can be helpful in finding relationships when learning something new.

Teachers can influence pattern in these ways:

- Presenting schemas as advance organizers
- Embedding skills in real-world contexts
- Integrating skills across the curriculum
- Ensuring that new learning has real-world application

2. Emotions Are Critical to the Learning Process

Emotions are inextricable from the learning process (Ornstein & Sobel, 1987). Most learning depends on our state of mind, emotions, goals, and personal sense of confidence. Emotions facilitate the storage of memories and help in the recall process.

Implications for Learning

The emotional climate set for the classroom is crucial to student success. It is essential that teachers and students are supportive and cooperative. As previously mentioned, a positive climate is necessary for optimal learning.

3. Learning Involves the Entire Physiology

Learning is a natural process (Smilkstein, 2003). The brain constantly looks for new information, is curious, and is self-perpetuating if given the opportunity. Relevance, personal meaning, or novelty, if present, helps the process along. Our experiences help promote neuron growth and brain development (Diamond, 1988). The brain is very susceptible to either positive or negative experiences. To grow dendrites, students need enriched environments that include stimulation of all senses—visual, auditory, and kinesthetic modes of learning. This premise also supports the five natural learning systems (Given, 2002) and tends to be true for all learners regardless of their learning styles or multiple intelligence strengths.

Implications for Learning

Although there are some common themes in terms of the brain's functioning, each brain is unique based on life experiences and emotional situations. Not all students are at the same level of maturation at the same chronological age. There may be up to five years' difference in maturation between any two "average students." Attributing delays based on chronological age may not be accurate but may cause undo anxiety and stress in students and parents if expectations are based on chronological growth.

4. Searching for Meaning

The search for meaning is a basic survival instinct. The brain recognizes the familiar and also looks for novelty (O'Keefe & Nadel, 1978). This occurs while we are awake or asleep. It is impossible to shut this search down. The best we can do is channeling this quest and helping the learner focus by using contracts, projects, questions, and inquiry.

Implications for Learning

This challenges teachers' ability to structure an environment that is familiar yet has novelty, challenge, and investigative capacity. Programs must build on the familiar while also creating a sense of wonderment and challenge. Engagement in reading, writing, and speaking with interesting and relevant topics is crucial to intrigue the learner.

5. Learning Is Social

The need to connect, associate, collaborate, and cooperate is prevalent in all humans as well as other species (Panksepp, 1998). However, some of us have more of a need for social interaction. We tend to place value on independence and interdependence as a positive human trait (Covey, 1989). Basically, students need to feel that they belong, are contributing members of a group, and are accepted and respected.

Implications for Learning

Because social interactions are such an innate part of human nature, it would be counterproductive to outlaw oral communication in the classroom. This can be especially frustrating for those interpersonal or "puppy" learners who need to dialogue and share ideas and "talk out their thinking" with someone else.

6. Learning Involves Conscious and Unconscious Attention

The brain is continually concerned with making sense of the world (Sylwester, 1995). Everything from body language, classroom climate, and physical environment, including décor and orderliness is included in peripheral stimuli. This is subconscious, but the brain still registers it and reacts to it. There is a climate that permeates the classroom and the school that is picked up by students and teachers alike.

Implications for Learning

Environment and subtleties in the classroom affect the learners. Tone of voice, cheerful displays in classrooms with the use of support structures such as charts, diagrams, word walls, and visuals help students with their learning. The teacher's concern for his or her students and personal enthusiasm for learning influences students at the unconscious level and relates both the joy and value of learning. The brain picks up subconscious messages and responds in a positive or negative way as a result of that information. What we do screams louder than what we say.

7. Every Brain Is Unique

Although every brain operates in basically the same way, we know that each one is unique. This is a result of nature and nurture (heredity and environment). We each have a genetic makeup and various experiences and environments that have influenced and constructed our brains differently over time.

Implications for Learning

These differences play out through learning styles and different strengths in areas of intelligence. Circumstances, including culture, poverty, first language, and special needs, add diversity to the learners' individual profile.

THE TWO HEMISPHERES OF THE BRAIN

Research from Roger Sperry (1968) identified two different hemispheres of the brain and two different ways of processing information. One side seems to be dominant in each of us, and research also indicates that gender plays a role in hemisphere dominance as well (Baron-Cohen, 2003; Blum, 1997; Gurian, Henley, & Trueman, 2001; Havers, 1995; Moir & Jessel, 1989; Rich, 2000; Taylor, 2002; Witelson, 2004). Figures 1.2 and 1.3 itemize the processes linked with each hemisphere and suggest what the hemisphere dominance looks like in the classroom. Figures 1.4 and 1.5 detail the structural and performance differences linked to male and female brain hemispheres.

This is not to say that we should do only one activity or the other based on the student's gender, but we should provide a full range of activities that develop both sides of the brain (see Figure 1.6). Sometimes we can ask girls to engage in activities that require more manipulation, with opportunities to build, construct, calculate, and design. And sometimes boys can be required by design to verbally describe what they are doing; it is easier for them to vocalize when actively involved in a task. There is more blood flow to the cerebellum (the motor brain) at that time, and thus their vocabulary will be greater.

Figure 1.2   Brain Processes Linked to Left and Right Hemispheres

Left Hemisphere	Right Hemisphere
Controls the right side of the body	Controls the left side of the body
Logical use of information	Spontaneous reaction to information
Analytical with data	Intuitively responds to information (commonsense approach)
Time sensitive and aware	Does not consider time
Deals with life sequentially	Deals with life randomly
Organizes information	Diffuses information
Uses formal and systematic ways to deal with information and materials	Uses spur of the moment to deal with information and materials
Processes from whole to parts and reorganizes the whole (sees the trees)	Sees the big picture or the whole (sees the forest)
Responds to verbal communication both receiving and expressing	Responds to body language, touch, and intonational pitch
Music: writes scientifically	Music: responds to sound and tone
Practical and factual	Focuses on ideas, theories, and uses imagery
Generates spoken language	Interprets language
Control emotions, feelings	Free with feelings and emotions
Uses mathematics and computations	Uses intuition to perceive and estimates
Responds to abstract-oriented thinking	Responds to sensory-oriented thinking
Concrete, explicit, and precise	Symbolic and metaphorical

NOTE: To read more about this, see Carter (1998) and Gazzaniga (1998a, 1998b).

Figure 1.3   Preferences in the Classroom Related to Dominant Hemisphere

Left-Hemisphere Dominance	Right-Hemisphere Dominance
• Prefers facts	• Prefers possibilities
• Relies on logical analysis and systemic solutions	• Relies on intuition and hunches to solve problems
• Repetition/rehearsal	• Likes inventive options
• Traditional use of materials	• Innovative use of materials
• Order	• Random and haphazard
• Precision	• Spontaneity
• Models	• Elaborates on the original
• Demonstrations	• Expands on ideas given
• Expectations drive learning	• Curiosity drives learning
• Relies on feedback for success	• Suggests options
• Clear directions	• Jumps into task without directions
• Instructions from teacher (auditory)	• Experiments with ideas
• Seeks approval	• Shows others their accomplishments
• Likes multiple-choice test questions	• Prefers essay questions on test

Figure 1.4   Gender Differences: Structural

Male	Female
Higher percentage of gray matter in left.	Same amount of gray matter in both hemispheres.
Have more neurons in the cerebral cortex.	Females have more connections between the neurons in the same size space.
Left hemisphere has language areas for both males and females.	Females have an active processor in their right brain as well.
Boys have less blood flow in their brains.	Female corpus callosum (connecting the left and right hemispheres) is generally larger than males (almost 25% in adolescence).
Boys' brains "renew, recharge and reorient" through the process of a *rest state*	Girls reorient without a *rest state*.
More cortical area devoted to spatial processing.	In the temporal lobes, girls have more neural connectors than boys. Thus they store more sensory details, often have a greater ability to listen, and pick up intonation clues while listening.
	The hippocampus in girls is generally larger as well. Because it processes memory storage, girls have a learning advantage, especially in language arts.
	Girls' prefrontal lobes are more active at an earlier age, and this decreases the impulsivity often apparent in male behavior.
Boys have less serotonin and also less oxytocin (human bonding chemical). They are thus more physically impulsive and sometimes less demonstrative of affection.	Girls generally have higher levels of serotonin in the blood, which makes them less impulsive.

NOTE: Based on information compiled from multiple sources, including the work of Witelson (2004), Moir and Jessel (1989), Taylor (2002), Havers (1995), Gurian et al. (2001), Rich (2000), Baron-Cohen (2003), and Blum (1997).

Figure 1.5   Gender Differences: Performance

Male	Female
Males use more cortical area for spatial and mechanical functioning.	Females use generally more cortical area for emotive and verbal processing.
Perform better on spatial tasks such as	Perform better on
• three-dimensional rotation of objects, • motor skills, • noticing embedded shapes, • throwing accuracy, • mathematical reasoning.	• perceptual speed tests, • verbal fluency, memory, • sequence, • identifying specific attributes of an object, • manual precise tasks (finger dexterity), • mathematical calculations.
Males lateralize and tend to compartmentalize their learning.	Females are better at noticing a variety of emotions (temporal lobes) in others and use a greater amount of their limbic system to do so. Multitasking is easier for girls. They make transitions easier from one thing to another. They are more able to focus.

NOTE: Based on information compiled from multiple sources, including the work of Witelson (2004), Moir and Jessel (1989), Rich (2000), and Blum (1997).

Figure 1.6   Teaching to Gender Differences

Teaching Boys	Teaching Girls
• Offer as many kinesthetic, hands-on activities as possible: manipulatives, construction, projects, experiments.	• Encourage physical activity to develop gross motor skills.
• Provide tasks that include fine motor (not as highly developed in males) as well as gross motor that is often preferred by males (physical theater).	• Use materials to promote sensory engagement and spatial development. • Celebrate successes in spatial tasks.
• Keep oral instructions to a minimum and post for reference. Boys will zone out with too many verbal directions or explanations.	• Offer dilemmas, puzzles, and problems that challenge perceptual learning.
• Personalize a boy's space to increase feelings of belonging (desk, locker, etc.).	• Use team learning to foster social interaction and leadership skills.
• Foster empathy and social interaction.	• Encourage participation and sharing from quieter female students.

NOTE: To read more about this, see Gurian and Stevens (2004).

Offering opportunities for movement, work with hands-on manipulatives, and a variety of seating choices (chairs, rugs, cushions) also may help the brain focus. Figure 1.7 offers an inventory that may help people identify their dominant hemisphere. This should not be used to label them but to help them become more aware of and knowledgeable about themselves.

Figure 1.7   Left Hemisphere + Right Hemisphere = Whole Brain

Circle the numbers that are most like you.

 1. When I read about something new, I like pictures and diagrams.

 2. I prefer step-by-step directions and to solve problems logically.

 3. I get many ideas at once like "brainstorming."

 4. I like to learn by seeing and hearing.

 5. I remember people's faces better than their names.

 6. I can control my feelings.

 7. I like to create new and unique things.

 8. I can recall information quickly when I need it.

 9. I like to handle materials and examine things to understand them.

10. I learn new words and vocabulary quickly.

11. People would say I'm emotional.

12. I can learn easily with patience and by noticing details.

13. I picture ideas and review things in my "mind videos."

14. I like routines and have daily habits or rituals.

15. I rely on my intuition, and some people would call me spontaneous.

16. I can easily concentrate and focus when I need to.

17. I let a party "happen" and get involved with the people.

18. I plan a party down to the last detail.

19. I like to imagine new and interesting things.

20. I like true-and-false tests better than one where I have to write a lot.

21. I generally know what is going on and what everyone is doing.

22. I like to learn from the teacher.

23. I can see the whole jigsaw even though I have only a few pieces in place.

24. I can remember and describe details easily.

25. I sometimes lose track of time.

26. I usually manage time well.

27. I like group work and "catch" the mood of others.

28. I can concentrate well if I want to.

29. I like to learn by doing and touching.

30. I like to learn by listening and seeing.

_____ Number of odd numbers circled.

_____ Number of even numbers circled.

If you circled more odd numbers, you tend to be more right hemisphere oriented.

If you circled more even numbers, you tend to be more left hemisphere oriented.

WHOLE-BRAIN PROCESSING

Current research shows that the two hemispheres work more as a whole brain, with each one an integral part of the thinking/learning system, processing events so rapidly that they seem simultaneous. For example, the right hemisphere grasps the big picture, and the left hemisphere sorts out the details. Even the "hardheaded" thinking of the left hemisphere can be influenced by the intuition and aesthetics of the right hemisphere, resulting in a more balanced approach.

To integrate and stimulate the whole brain using each side, teachers can offer classroom activities that capitalize on both sides. For example, both hemispheres recognize words. The left hemisphere (Broca's area) interprets words and facilitates understanding by putting them in sequence and syntax. The right hemisphere relies on symbolism and the use of metaphors and analogies (one of the best practices suggested by Marzano, Pickering, & Pollock, 2001). To draw on the right hemisphere and use the whole brain, we want to use symbolism and metaphoric thinking, not just focus on conventions such as spelling, grammar, and writing.

Neuroscientist Elkhonon Goldberg (2001) offers us another theory of right-hemisphere/left-hemisphere organization. He suggests that the right hemisphere is organized to respond to new challenges and rapidly deal with situations that the brain has not previously encountered. He proposes that this is a function of the brain's survival plan that is the main purpose of the brain. A stranger's face offers unusual information that may suggest a threat. This image is quickly processed by the right side of the brain. Faces that are familiar are processed in the left hemisphere because they are not generally threatening. Both hemispheres of the brain are actively involved in most learning situations. The transfer of the information-processing function spills over from right to left when learning takes place. When we are learning new skills, the information processing is principally a right-hemisphere operation. The closer we come to mastery of a skill, processing is transferred from the right to the left side. The right hemisphere rapidly responds to new situations, but not necessarily with appropriate solutions. The left hemisphere then selects from the most promising solutions and designs strategies to be used in similar future situations.

A typical example of how this works is the acquisition of language. Youngsters may use a number of random verbal and nonverbal techniques to communicate their needs. This is a right-hemisphere job. As the child becomes more adept at communication, the left hemisphere selects the strategies that are successful and begins to construct a framework for both receiving and communicating language. It is important to use a wide range of strategies that specifically could be used for stimulating and engaging the right hemisphere and the left hemisphere. As we design learning activities that engage both hemispheres in the learning process, Figure 1.8 offers a variety of strategies worth trying.

Figure 1.8   Learning Activities That Strengthen Whole-Brain Processing

Left-Hemisphere Skills	Right-Hemisphere Skills
Keep the classroom orderly, materials and bulletin boards neat and current.	Provide multiple materials and resources.
Foster opportunities to read, write, and engage in numeracy activities.	Use hands-on experiences as well as role playing and simulations. Allow options for reading and writing.
Organize chalkboards and erase material that could become misconstrued with new material.	Use diagrams and illustrations as well as graphic organizers, charts, and timelines.
Provide agendas, expectations, and timelines.	Agendas may include visual mapping of concepts and topics of study.
Help students monitor their work, time, and successes.	Allow students to interact, discuss, and articulate their ideas.
Encourage logic and reasoning. Ask students to substantiate their thinking.	Use analogies and metaphors to help students make connections.
Encourage higher-order thinking.	Bring lessons to closure and integrate new information with past learning.

STRATEGIES FOR TEACHING TO THE RIGHT HEMISPHERE

Most classrooms are organized for and use strategies that appeal to the left hemisphere, such as concrete sequential directions, processes, and the like. To tap into the strengths of the right hemisphere and balance the thinking process, Cherry, Godwin, and Staples (1989) suggest imaging strategies, including visualization, guided imagery, and fantasy. Imaging strategies allow students to see images in the "mind's eye." This is a function of the right hemisphere and can be used to help right-dominant learners with their learning.

Visualization

Visualization is the ability to form a picture in the mind. It is visualization or visual thinking if the picture stems from the environment. It can be used for problem solving through the process of seeing the real objects or situations in the mind's eye. It sometimes helps to simplify the situation and often solves the problem. The learning may be made easier. The visualization acts as a visual aid that helps the situation.

Guided Imagery

Guided imagery starts as visualization from the environment but is taken to the next step by one's imagination. The facilitator, as to activities and connections, makes suggestions to students. Imagination takes over, and even though things are happening only in the mind, they seem to be happening in reality. All the senses can be evoked to further the imagination. Often, this is used to help students with their self-confidence and their self-esteem.

Fantasy

Although visualization and guided imagery come from the outside, fantasy comes from within. It requires a person to create ideas no matter how far out they are. They are like daydreams that help sort out desires, thoughts, and dilemmas. Fantasy may not solve all the problems, but they provide a way for young people to articulate situations and perhaps sort out some conflict and confusion. They also act as an "escape" or at least help achieve balance. We never know where fantasies will take us. They should be nurtured, talked about, and written down in a log or journal in a free-flow form.

Ten More Strategies

1. **Connecting:** Connect the new learning to a past experience that the learner has had at school, home, or other areas of their world.

2. **Focusing:** Before the learning, discuss with the students what they are going to be studying, how the processes will unfold, and what the expectations are. There may be an agenda map with symbols and pictures.

3. **Stimulating with visuals:** Be sure to use actual objects and materials if possible. Drawings and sketches, diagrams, illustrations, and photographs enhance the learning and develop deep understanding.

4. **Vocabulary building:** Build understanding of vocabulary by using language in a variety of situations to continually reinforce comprehension and retention.

5. **Hands on:** Provide manipulatives and real materials so that students can have tactile involvement with things related to the topic they are studying.

6. **Real-world usage:** Provide a "being there" experience and help students make connections between new ideas and things in their environment and day-to-day living.

7. **Innovation:** Challenge students by inspiring and motivating them to create new ideas and methods connected to a topic.

8. **Receiving feedback:** Use feedback in the form of questions, responses, and reinforcement to support these strategies.

9. **Repetition:** Rehearse and practice guided by feedback.

10. **Transfer:** As appropriate, help students to transfer their new learning to other problems and situations.

SUMMARY

It is essential that educators pay attention to what we know about the brain. We are working with brains every day. The more we know about the brain's organization, functions, and ways of operating and processing, the more we can thoughtfully design learning for our diverse students to ensure that they understand and store knowledge and skills for future use.

Learning Styles 2

It has been said that education is a people business, "a business about the diversity of people" (Guild & Garger, 1985). Eliot Eisner (1983) postulates that the difference between the art of teaching and just the craft is the teacher's willingness and ability to continue to garner additional teaching strategies and techniques to enhance a repertoire to reach all learners. This makes the teacher more of a facilitator than a technician.

UNDERSTANDING HOW PEOPLE PREFER TO LEARN

Recognizing that human beings differ is paramount to helping all students succeed. Learning styles theory generally looks at the "how" of teaching and learning rather than the "what." The *what* can be presented, studied, and ultimately learned through a variety of strategies and processes. A learning style, however, is a lens that we as educators can use to help differentiate instruction to appeal to, engage, and facilitate learning for different types of students who have different needs.

When we differentiate instruction to facilitate learning for students with diverse learning styles, we can adjust many things:

- Creating a classroom environment to match students' preferences
- Including instruction that appeals to all the senses
- Facilitating social interactions
- Differentiating levels of challenge and engagement
- Presenting material to appeal to auditory, visual, and kinesthetic modalities

Asking People How They Learn Best

It may seem somewhat simplistic to ask people how they learn best, but it can be a thinking and reflection exercise that helps both the learner and the teacher understand the individual better. Rita Smilkstein (2003), for example, suggests that people learn because they're born to learn and it is something that comes naturally to the brain.

If you take students through a guided reflection process, you might ask them the following:

1. Do you remember a time when you learned something well?

2. What was it? (Could be riding a bike, skate boarding, cooking, playing an instrument, keyboarding)

3. How did you learn it?

4. What were the steps?

5. How did you practice?

6. How did you feel about the learning process?

7. What made it so (good, fun, memorable)?

You will probably find that people say they learned something well when the following were true:

- They chose to learn it.
- They had fun learning.
- They got a sense of personal satisfaction from the experience.
- They were able to use the learning to enhance their lives.
- They enjoyed working with the instructor.

Generally, people don't mention a school subject, and their motivation is not usually a test score.

An emerging body of knowledge makes it clear that learners will learn best when they are put through activities that allow them to be comfortable in their own "learning skin." Bell (1986) suggests that students who learn in their preferred styles exhibit the following:

- Achieve better results
- Show more interest in the material
- Enjoy how they learned
- Want to learn more in the same way

Learning styles consider the cognitive, affective, physiological, and psychological needs of people—how they perceive and process information and how they engage with, interact with, and react to their surroundings and environment.

Figure 2.1   How People Think and Learn

Category	Characteristics
Cognition	People perceive information and develop understanding differently. **How do I know?**
Conceptualizing	People develop and form ideas differently. **How do I think?**
Affect	People feel and value differently. **How do I decide?**
Behavior	People behave or act differently. **How do I act?**

Guild and Garger (1985) suggest four categories that educators should be aware of in the classroom: cognition, conceptualizing, affect, and behavior. Figure 2.1 shows how those categories link up to the characteristics of "how" people think and learn. In most cases, learners will have a dominant style within a mode that is visual, auditory, or tactile/kinesthetic. Within those three modalities, their learning preferences will look different and often manifest in a variety of ways.

Visual Learners

- Create pictures in their mind and use images to remember
- Prefer reading, writing, making notes, and diagrams
- Accurately read body language and pick up on facial expressions
- Appreciate graphics and pictures
- Appreciate written instructions instead of oral ones
- "See" letters and words when spelling them
- Like to use drama and art
- Make lists and write things down
- Appreciate order and are distracted by clutter
- Attention may wander during verbal activities
- Exhibit upward eye movements, rapid speaking, and shallow breathing
- Use visual language when communicating, such as "It looks right to me" or "Don't you see?"

Auditory Learners

- Like to talk and listen to others
- Prefer verbal instructions
- Like to be read to

- Like to learn from lectures and audiotapes
- Hum, self-talk, or subvocalize when reading
- "Sound out" when they spell
- Practice aloud and learn by talking to themselves
- Like the telephone, radio, and chatting
- Exhibit sideways eye movements, even speech, and mid-chest breathing
- Use auditory language, such as "It sounds right" or "Listen to this"

Kinesthetic Learners

- Often use movement and are action oriented
- Seem to gesture when speaking and fidget
- Tap or drum on desk
- Seem to be impulsive
- Don't choose to read if possible
- Like to act out concepts and "do" things
- Have to write words as they spell (find spelling challenging)
- Prefer sports and dancing
- Solve problems while moving
- Touch while they communicate
- Exhibit downward eye movements, deep breathing, and slow speech
- Use language of action and feelings, such as "I feel that it's right" or "Now I get it"

How Preferences Affect Learning

Ken and Rita Dunn (1987) have developed a learning styles profile that examines how classroom factors affect visual, auditory, and kinesthetic learners (see Figure 2.2). The factors they cover are listed here:

Environmental

- Light (soft/bright, natural/artificial)
- Temperature (hot/cold)
- Sound (noisy/quiet)
- Design (formal/informal)

Emotional

- Responsibility (takes responsibility/lacks responsibility)
- Structure (generates ideas easily/needs assistance)
- Motivation (extrinsic/intrinsic)
- Persistence (lacks persistence/keeps on task)

Figure 2.2   How Classroom Factors Affect Visual, Auditory, and Kinesthetic Learners

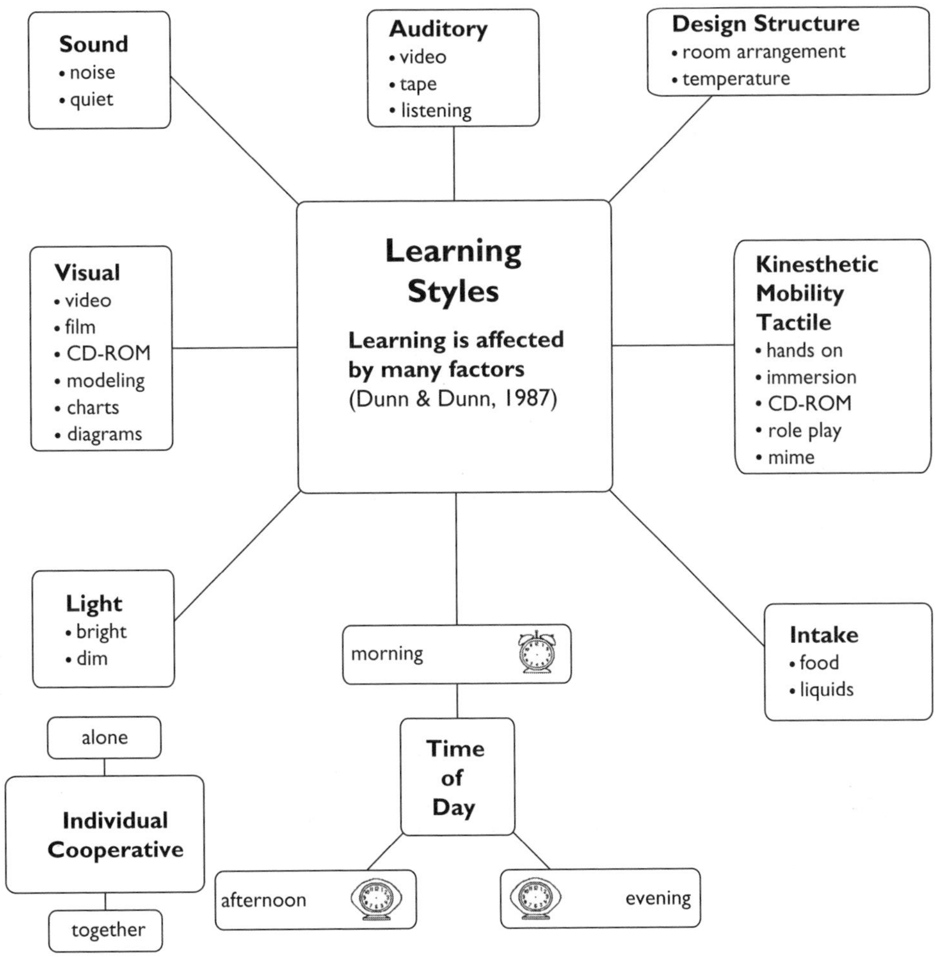

Sociological

- Likes to work
  Alone
  Partners
  Small group
  Friends
  Varied

Physical

- Time (morning/afternoon)
- Perceptual (auditory/verbal)

- Mobility (sits in seat/likes to walk around)
- Intake (with or without food)

Psychological

- Global/analytical (big picture/sees the details)
- Hemisphericity (right/left)
- Impulsive/reflective (no forethought to action/thinking before action)

ASSESSING HOW PEOPLE PREFER TO LEARN

To help teachers become more aware of student preferences for their optimal learning conditions, we can survey our learners. We can also observe them, paying attention to the conscious and unconscious cues they offer us. The following are a variety of assessment tools to use with your learners:

Learner surveys: Figures 2.3 and 2.4 offer two separate surveys that can be distributed and used for self-assessment and reflection about preferences.

Figure 2.3   Preference Survey I

Check the answers that match your learning preferences.

1. Where would you prefer to study or do homework?
   - ☐ In your room
   - ☐ In front of the TV
   - ☐ With music on
   - ☐ In a quiet place
   - ☐ On the floor
   - ☐ At a desk
   - ☐ Kitchen table
   - ☐ Using a computer
   - ☐ With a desk lamp or a window light
   - ☐ Alone
   - ☐ With a friend

2. When are you more alert?
   - ☐ In the morning
   - ☐ In the afternoon
   - ☐ In the evening

3. When you don't complete something is it because
   ☐ It's boring
   ☐ I can't do it
   ☐ I forgot
   ☐ I'd rather do . . .

4. What do you enjoy most in school? Why?

   _____

   _____

5. Where do you like to sit in class?
   ☐ Near the wall
   ☐ Near the door
   ☐ Near the front
   ☐ Near the back
   ☐ Near a window

6. If something is new to you do you want to
   ☐ Have someone to explain it to you?
   ☐ Watch a directional video?
   ☐ See a demonstration?
   ☐ Read about it?
   ☐ Just try it?

7. Do you prefer to work
   ☐ Alone?
   ☐ With a friend?
   ☐ With a partner?
   ☐ In a group?

8. When you work do you
   ☐ Like to snack?
   ☐ Never think about food?
   ☐ Have to have something to sip on?
   ☐ Have to move around?
   ☐ Have to be cozy?
   ☐ Have to be comfortable?

I've always known . . .

I never knew . . .

This helps me because, to . . .

I'm going to . . .

Figure 2.4   Preference Survey 2

Circle the number for your preferred answer to finish each statement.

1. I learn easiest
what I hear   1
what I read   2
what I do   3
by myself   4
talking with others   5

2. I'd rather work
with someone else   5
in a quiet place   4

3. I'd prefer
to read a story   2
to listen to a story   1
to make my own plan   4
to build a project   3

4. I get more done
alone   4
with others   5

5. I'd rather
get directions from someone   1
read how to get there   2
just do it   3

6. If I have to memorize I do it by
reading it many times   2
writing it out   3
repeating it again and again   1
having my friend ask me questions   5

7. I learn best when I can
talk with others about it   5
can concentrate by myself   4

8. When I study
I move around a lot   3
I read things over   2
I think it through by myself   4
I like to study with a friend   5
I talk things out   1
I make notes and diagrams   2

9. When I listen to the teacher I prefer to
just listen   1
take notes and make pictures   2
doodle and draw   3
talk to someone about the ideas   5
think about it later when I'm alone   4

10. I express my emotions
by my tone of voice | 1
by my body actions | 3
with my face | 2

11. If I'm angry, I often
become quiet | 4
tell people about it | 1
grit my teeth, stomp off | 3
talk to a friend | 5

12. In my free time I like to
watch TV or read | 2
stay in my room | 4
hang out with my friends | 5
go for a walk or run, play a game | 3
listen to music | 1

Total the number of each number and put on the line below.

1_____ 2_____ 3_____ 4_____ 5_____

A high number of 1's indicates a more auditory preference.

A high number of 2's indicates a more visual preference.

A high number of 3's indicates a more kinesthetic preference.

A high number of 4's indicates a more individual preference.

A high number of 5's indicates a more interpersonal preference.

Listening to students: Figures 2.5 and 2.6 list words and phrases that often reveal whether learners prefer visual, auditory, or kinesthetic learning modes, even when the words are used at an unconscious level.

Observing students' body cues: Figure 2.7 itemizes how a person's pattern of accessing cues through posture, voice, and motion can signal preferences.

Observing students' eye cues: Bandler and Grinder (1979) initiated this research into how eye movement can give clues to cognitive processing. If we watch a student's eyes carefully when we ask a question, we can receive clues to the type of sensory processing taking place: You can know

Figure 2.5   Words That Signal Learner Preferences

Visual	Auditory	Kinesthetic
Look	Listen	Feel
See	Hear	Touch
Observe	Speak	In touch
Clear	Talk	Firm
Watch	Clear as a bell	Heavy
Viewpoint	Tell myself	Grasp
Point of view	Told	Hurt
Focus	Say	Raise an issue
Mirror	Loud	Soft touch
Insight	Well said	Itchy
Image	So to speak	Lightweight
Reflect	Drum it in	Gut feeling
Fuzzy	Answer	Relaxed
Vivid	Low key	Sleep on it
Hazy	Pitch	Touchy
Foresight	Tune in	Shoulder the blame
Eyeball	Tone	Come to grips
Picture	Volume	Let go

Figure 2.6   Phrases That Signify Learner Preferences

Visual	Auditory	Kinesthetic
I see what you're saying.	Tell me what . . .	Let me throw out this idea.
Let me be clear about . . .	What do you say?	I feel stuck . . .
Let's focus on . . .	It sounds to me . . .	This is rough going . . .
Picture this . . .	In other words . . .	Let's bounce this
I get the picture . . .	I'll call you later.	around . . .
Show me what you mean . . .	It's no laughing matter.	I'm sinking . . .
Another way of looking at	You're tuning me out.	Run that by me . . .
it is . . .	Listen to me . . .	You have closed your mind.
What do you see?	That rang a bell . . .	Put a lid on it for now.
Do you see what I mean?	Voice your ideas . . .	It all fell into place.
It's crystal clear . . .	I don't like the sound of . . .	Let's pool our ideas.
It looks as though . . .	How does this sound?	If we pull together . . .
I'll show you . . .	The tone of your voice . . .	Jump to it.
Let's take another look at . . .	There's a lot to tell . . .	Get a move on.
		He let me down.

Figure 2.7   Body Accessing Cues That Signal Learner Preferences

	Visual	**Auditory**	**Kinesthetic**
Posture	Holds shoulders higher and tenser	Shoulders seem to be at average level	Shoulders tend to be lower and relaxed
Voice tone	Higher pitch	In between	Lower pitch
Rate of voice	Faster rate	In between	Slower rate
Muscle tone	More tense	In between	More relaxed
Hand/arm movement	Higher in air	In between	Lower in air

Figure 2.8   Eye Movements That Signal Learner Preferences

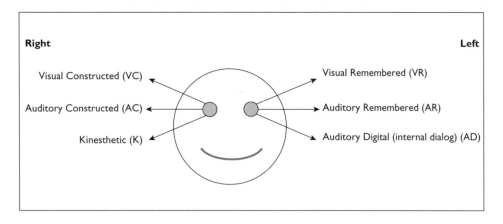

whether the answer is recalled or remembered (looking left), created or fantasy (looking right), truth or recall. This can help you know when you are hearing the truth. In addition, you will know the sensory mode being used: visual (looking up), auditory (looking to the side), or kinesthetic (looking down) (see Figure 2.8). This is true for right-handed students. If they are left-handed, the opposite will occur.

Observing students' choices: Students often choose learning tasks and activities depending on their dominant style: visual, auditory, or kinesthetic. Figure 2.9 lists typical learner actions in the left column and learner preferences in the right column.

LEARNING STYLES THEORY

For many years, experts have been developing and sharing a variety of theories that identify and explain people's learning styles. Learning styles

Figure 2.9   Learner Choices

What They Do!	What They Want to Do!
Visual Learners	**Visual Learners**
Like to look at books Like order and materials organized Can find items easily Detect errors easily Can find work and get down to business Watch others to see what to do Enjoy puzzles Read faces	Draw pictures to represent ideas Use games: matching, puzzles, Use visual cues to remember Have a "being there" experience; take a field trip Use visualization to see pictures in their minds Use graphics and flowcharts Use video for review
Auditory Learners	**Auditory Learners**
Chatter constantly Like to "have the floor" (audience) Often good spellers Like to tell stories and tales Can recall and recount conversation Like music, rap, rhyme Good at memorization	Give directions aloud Discuss what they are learning Use games (verbal), puzzles, scrambles, riddles, and songs Use a tape recorder Work with study buddies Do choral reading Teach others for clarification
Kinesthetic Learners	**Kinesthetic Learners**
They move Are touchy, feely Like hands-on work for everything Handle other people (bumps, high 5's) Examine and manipulate materials Often well coordinated Always doing something while listening	Have opportunities to move and handle materials Trace and highlight Act out concepts and stories Make models or do experiments Write or draw while listening Walk while thinking Use hands and arms to express and explain Imagine themselves in the situation Simulate

tell us how learner preferences relate to how they acquire, process, and learn new information and skills. This book includes several well-known learning styles theories and profiles introduced by educators and psychologists, including Carl Jung, Anthony Gregorc, David Kolb, Bernice McCarthy, Don Lowry, Richard Strong, Harvey Silver, and J. R. Hanson. Throughout the chapter, I use four commonplace symbols to organize core aspects of each profile: a beach ball, a clipboard, a puppy, and a microscope. Introduced in *Differentiated Instructional Strategies: One Size Doesn't Fit All* (Gregory & Chapman, 2002), these four symbols can help us synthesize and align key principles from the learning styles for instructional planning and differentiation.

Figure 2.10 Gregorc's Learning Styles: Learner Attributes

Style	Attributes	
Concrete Random	**Concrete** Likes practicality Needs models Sees "big picture" Likes trial and error	**Random** Divergent thinkers Intuitive leaps Appreciates choice Looks for alternatives
Concrete Sequential	**Concrete** Likes lists Likes hands-on activities Likes to learn	**Sequential** Procedural, timelines Likes details Appreciates order

Abstract Random	**Abstract**
	Feelings and emotions
	Needs nonthreatening
	  environment
	Knows answer but
	  can't always explain
		Random
		Flexible and spontaneous
		Seeks variety
		Visual imagination

Abstract Sequential	**Abstract** Needs time to process Applies analytical strategies Likes investigation and analysis	**Sequential** Appreciates order Rational and logical Needs personal connections

Gregorc's Learning Style Channels

Anthony Gregorc's (1982) theory of thinking is based on two variables: the way we order the world (random or sequential) and the way we view the world (abstract or concrete). By combining these variables, Gregorc created four learning styles with learner attributes as shown in Figure 2.10: concrete random, concrete sequential, abstract random, and abstract sequential. Using Gregorc's groupings to differentiate learner preferences, we can then match learning activities to learner styles (see Figure 2.11).

Kolb's Experiential Learning Profile

David Kolb's (1984) learning style profile includes four groups of learners: divergers, assimilators, convergers, and accommodators. Their characteristics are shown in Figure 2.12.

Figure 2.11   Gregorc's Learning Styles: Learning Activities

Concrete Random	Concrete Sequential
Computer work Games Independent study Open-ended problem solving Exploration and good information Written assignments and reading Creating and making Simulations	Field trips Workbooks Study guides Manuals Directions and instructions Application of skills Performance evaluation Hands-on activities
Abstract Random	Abstract Sequential
Interviewing people Role-playing feelings Songs, letters, poetry Movies, films, music Guest speakers Visuals and art Peer teaching and tutoring Personalizing situations	Researching background information Establishing criteria Explaining reasons and rationale Appreciates lectures Synthesizing findings Debates, panel discussions Analytical essays Reading thoroughly

Figure 2.12   Kolb's Experiential Learning Profile

Divergers	• Value positive, caring environment • Appreciate comfortable surroundings • Like dialogue and conversation • Enjoy interaction and sharing thinking with others • Like to explore alternatives • Enjoy the pursuit of learning
Assimilators	• Seek investigation • Like to read and research • Have the patience to delve into the learning • Enjoy abstract content • Like to learn from past experiences and from experts
Convergers	• Desire to learn what is practical and useful • Like to identify relevant information and organize it • Appreciate clear goals and timelines • Need to know expectations and criteria for success
Accommodators	• Want to try out new things and ideas • Like to "shake up" their thinking and others' • Appreciate opportunities to be creative • Are flexible, risk takers • Often want to do things their own way

Lowry's Colors Inventory

Don Lowry (1979) developed a learning style inventory that uses four colors to typify each learning style—blue being the harmonious learner, green the curious learner, gold the responsible learner, and orange the adventurous learner. Figure 2.13 shows the attributes of each color in Lowry's model.

McCarthy's 4MAT Model

Noted educator Bernice McCarthy (1990, 2000) synthesized the work of theorists Kolb, Lotas, Jung, Fisher(s), Gregorc, Wetzig, and Merrill as well as research on brain hemisphericity to develop her 4MAT system. McCarthy identifies four types of learners:

- Imaginative learner: sensing, watching, and asking, "Why?"
- Analytical learner: watching, thinking, and asking, "What?"
- Common sense learner: Thinking and trying and asking, "How does it work?"
- Dynamic learner: Trying, sensing, and asking, "What can this become?"

Figure 2.13   Lowry's Colors Learning Style Inventory

Blue—Harmonious	This temperament is typified by completeness, calm, and sense of belonging. Blues like a harmonious, balanced, and tension-free environment. Blue symbolizes security, comfort, and authenticity. They search for meaning and enjoy close relationships and have a spiritual side to their nature.
Green—Curious	This temperament is typified by growth, abundance, and development. Greens like to feel competent and capable. They strive for perfection and seek to reach their true potential. They enjoy complexity and are analytical. They experience depth of feelings but don't like to openly express their feelings.
Gold—Responsible	This temperament is typified by loyalty, security, and stability. Golds feel responsible and enjoy service to others. They prefer order and tradition. They like to be the backbone of society by fulfilling their obligations and caring for others.
Orange—Adventurous	This temperament is typified by activity, vitality, and energy. Oranges like spontaneity and action as the moment dictates. They are often seen as impulsive and hands on when it comes to problem solving. They take control in a crisis and get joy from doing so.

Figure 2.14 summarizes the characteristics of the four learning types, and Figure 2.15 shows how the 4MAT model works with all four learning types through four quadrants of a circle.

Beginning the lesson in Quadrants 1 and 2 with the discussion method and the information method, Types 1 and 2 are more dependent and motivated by the teacher. These learners appreciate teacher involvement

Figure 2.14 McCarthy's 4MAT Model: Learning Types

Type 1: Imaginative Learner Experiencing Asks, "Why?"	• Wants to know *why* they should learn it • Asks questions, predicts, and asks what if? • Questions content and purposes • Seeks to understand • Uses feelings and reflections • Wants to make connections • Seeks alternative solutions
Type 2: Analytical Learner Conceptualizing Asks, "What?"	• Seeks facts and information • Wants to organize information • Works systematically • Likes organizers (advanced and graphic) • Wants clear purpose, directions, and expectations • Needs time for reflection before action • Asks *what* are the parts, components?
Type 3: Common Sense Learner Applying Asks, "How?"	• Desires practicality and usability • Likes to try things out and use new ideas • Want information to be applicable to life • Uses comparison (compare and contrast) to make sense of new information • Interested in *"how to"*
Type 4: Dynamic Learner Creating Asks, "What next?"	• Want to create with knowledge and skills • Wants freedom to risk new ways of thinking • Wants to think "outside the box" • Often wants to forge ahead alone but will work with others • Dislikes the monotonous or routine • Likes to dive into learning and apply their ideas • Asks *What can this be used for or become?*

NOTE: For more information about the 4MAT method, see McCarthy (1990, 2000).

Figure 2.15   McCarthy's 4MAT Model: Learning Quadrants

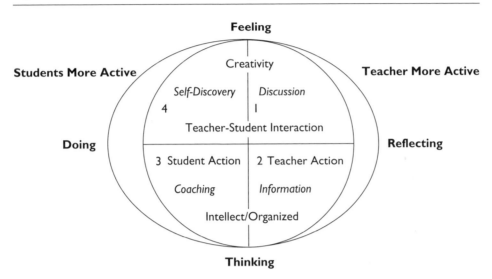

and direction in roles such as motivator and information giver. In contrast, Types 3 and 4, the coaching method and self-discovery method, prefer the teacher as coach, facilitator, evaluator, remediator, and resource. With Types 1 and 2, the teacher is more active. With Types 3 and 4 the student is more active (and growing more dendrites).

As the lesson or unit progresses through all four quadrants, all four styles of learners can have their needs and preferences addressed and satisfied (Figure 2.16). Differentiation can take place naturally at each stage of learning, beginning with the first quadrant and then proceeding around the cycle to uncover new learning opportunities in a variety of perspectives (Figure 2.17).

Carl Jung's Psychological Types

Swiss psychologist Carl Jung (1923) suggested that there are four personality types (psychological types) that we as humans present. He suggested that there are two main cognitive functions: how we absorb information—perception—and how we process information—judgment. Jung then divided those functions as follows:

Perception is acquired through

S: Sensing or use of the senses

N: Intuition or through conceptualizing the "big picture"

Figure 2.16   McCarthy's 4MAT System: Learner Likes and Dislikes

	Likes	Dislikes
Type 1: Imaginative Learner Experiencing Asks, "Why?"	Group work Pass/fail grading Self-evaluation Observation Participation grades Time to reflect	Timed tests Debates Computer-assisted instruction "Go for it"
Type 2: Analytical Learner Conceptualizing Asks, "What?"	Written tests Essays Multiple-choice tests Concepts and ideas Collecting data Comments and feedback	Pass/fail grading Role playing Subjective tests Group grades

Type 3: Common Sense Learner
Applying
Asks, "How?"
	Field trips
	Movement and
	  hands on
	Skills-oriented
	  evaluation
	Practical applications
	Labs
		Memorizing
		Group work
		Writing assignments
		Peer evaluation, feelings
		Being given answers

Type 4: Dynamic Learner Creating Asks, "What next?"	Open-ended questions Interdisciplinary units Flexible demands Looking for patterns Self-discovery projects	Repetition and drill Reflecting, inactivity Assignments without choice

Figure 2.17 McCarthy's 4MAT Model: Differentiated Learning

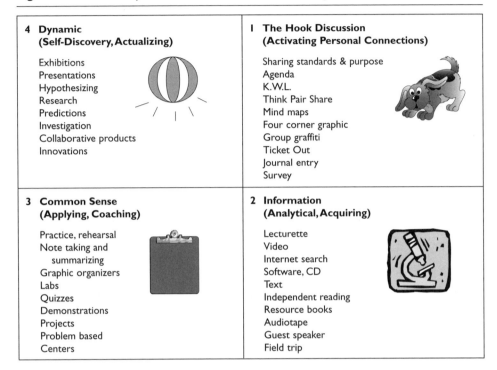

4 **Dynamic** **(Self-Discovery, Actualizing)**	1 **The Hook Discussion** **(Activating Personal Connections)**
Exhibitions Presentations Hypothesizing Research Predictions Investigation Collaborative products Innovations	Sharing standards & purpose Agenda K.W.L. Think Pair Share Mind maps Four corner graphic Group graffiti Ticket Out Journal entry Survey
3 **Common Sense** **(Applying, Coaching)**	2 **Information** **(Analytical, Acquiring)**
Practice, rehearsal Note taking and summarizing Graphic organizers Labs Quizzes Demonstrations Projects Problem based Centers	Lecturette Video Internet search Software, CD Text Independent reading Resource books Audiotape Guest speaker Field trip

Judgment is done by

T: Thinking or connective logic

F: Feeling or personal connections and meaningful relevancy

In Jung's (1923) words, these types "correspond to the obvious means by which consciousness obtains its orientation to experience: sensation (sensing) tells you that something exists, thinking tells you what it is; feeling tells you whether it is agreeable or not; and intuition tells you from whence it comes and where it is going" (p. 481).

Silver and Hanson's Learning Styles Profile

Harvey Silver and J. R. Hanson (2000) developed a profile from the theories of Carl Jung.

Interpersonal Learners (SF)

These learners like to interact with other learners, discuss, socialize, and thrive on teacher approval and nurturing. They want teachers to make the learning relevant to them so that the learning is personalized and meaningful.

Understanding Learners (NT)

These learners like to analyze, compare, contrast, classify, and summarize their learning. They appreciate quality information and then a chance to digest, probe, and think logically and analytically.

Mastery Learners (ST)

These learners like to practice, observe, describe, and memorize new learning to be successful. They like information presented to them and like to practice 'til perfect.

Self-Expressive Learners (NF)

These learners like originality, spontaneity, and elaborative thinking. They like choices and are creative, innovative learners.

LEARNING STYLES IN ACTION

Analogies for Learning Style Synthesis

Using the puppy, microscope, beach ball, and clipboard symbols to organize core aspects of learning styles theory can support analogous thinking to make it easier for us to remember and apply the principles of learning styles. Figure 2.18 shows a matrix of the different theories side by side, and Figure 2.19 synthesizes learner attributes from the different theories into four primary learning styles represented by our symbolic objects.

Teachers can consider using a self-reflection inventory as shown in Figure 2.20 as a way to help students identify their own learning styles and to collect data for teacher use in planning. Ask the students to read each statement in Figure 2.20 and to circle the numbers of the statements that are most like them. The inventory includes a scoring guide that can help them identify their learner preferences related to beach balls, puppies, clipboards, and microscopes.

Figures 2.21 to 2.24 will then allow us to examine all four learning styles individually as to their innate abilities, when they learn best, what is challenging for them, and what they need to work at. It's not that we want to label students or identify their learning styles and then cater to

Figure 2.18   Matrix of Learning Styles

	Gregorc	Kolb	Colors	4MAT	Silver/Strong/ Hanson
Puppy	**Abstract Random** • Imaginative • Emotional • Holistic	**Diverger** Value positive, caring environments that are attractive, comfortable, and safe	**Blue** Best in open, interactive environments where teachers add a personal touch	**Type 1** Feel and reflect Create and reflect on experience	**Interpersonal** Appreciates concrete ideas and social interaction to process and use knowledge **SF**
Microscope	**Abstract Sequential** • Intellectual • Analytical • Theoretical	**Assimilator** Avid readers who seek to learn Patience for research Value concepts	**Green** Best when exposed to overall theory and interpretation	**Type 2 Analytical** Reflect and think Observers who appreciate lecture	**Understanding** Prefers to explore ideas and use reason and logic based on evidence **NT**
Clipboard	**Concrete Sequential** • Task oriented • Efficient • Detailed	**Converger** Values what is useful and relevant Immediacy and organizing the essential is important	**Gold** Best in well structured and clearly defined situations	**Type 3 Common Sense** Think and do Active, practical Make things work	**Mastery** Absorbs information concretely and processes step by step **ST**
Beach ball	**Concrete Random** • Divergent • Experiential • Inventive	**Accommodator** Likes to try new ideas Values creativity, flexibility and opportunities	**Orange** Best in competitive situations especially with action	**Type 4 Dynamic** Creating and acting Usefulness and application of learning	**Self-Expressive** Uses feelings to construct new ideas Produces original or unique materials **NF**

those styles. It's that we want to be aware of what all learners need and consider how we can build in differentiation for those needs in the classroom.

We also want students to recognize their own styles so that they are conscious of their strengths and can advocate for what they need to be successful and engaged in the learning. Knowing themselves also helps them to understand that when they are frustrated or anxious, it may be related to their styles. This will also allow and facilitate the reflective theater to be used.

Figure 2.19   Synthesis of Learning Styles Theories

SF	Tendencies	
Sensing/Feeling **Abstract Random** **Diverger** **Blue** **Imaginative** **Interpersonal** **Social/Emotional Theater**	*Sensing* Focuses on what works Enjoys application Realistic Careful about facts Accepts current reality Works steadily Can oversimplify	*Feeling* Likes harmony and works at it Likes praise Is sympathetic Dislikes unpleasant things Enjoys pleasing others Takes an interest in people Considers people as well as task
NT	Tendencies	
Intuitive/Thinking **Abstract Sequential** **Assimilator** **Green** **Analytical** **Understanding** **Cognitive/Reflective Theater**	*Intuitive* Likes challenges Looks at possibilities Likes variety Enjoys new options Moves quickly Has bursts of energy	*Thinking* Appreciates logic and reason Responds to people's ideas Needs fair treatment Firm and tough-minded Not attuned to feelings Has a talent for analyzing
ST	Tendencies	
Sensing/Thinking **Concrete Sequential** **Converger** **Gold** **Common Sense** **Mastery** **Cognitive/Physical** **Theater**	*Sensing* Focuses on what works Enjoys application Realistic Careful about facts Accepts current reality Works steadily Can oversimplify	*Thinking* Likes a plan Likes things settled and complete Finishing is important Satisfied with a judgment Essentials are important Schedule is necessary Uses lists and agendas
NF	Tendencies	
Intuitive/Feeling **Concrete** **Random** **Accommodator** **Orange** **Dynamic** **Self-Expressive/** **Physical Theater**	*Intuitive* Likes challenges Looks at possibilities Likes variety Enjoys new options Moves quickly Has bursts of energy	*Feeling* Likes open-ended questions Adapts to change Has trouble with decisions May start too many projects Postpones the unpleasant Responds to pressure

Beach Ball Learners

Jennifer was my beach ball learner. From Day 1, she was animated, active, and expressive. She was always curious and excited about learning. She always had a new game or a "better way to build a mouse trap." She loved school at first. The excitement of new territory to explore and all the adventures she hopes for encouraged her each day. Early elementary school was great. She had innovative and stimulating kindergarten, first-grade and second-grade teachers who capitalized on her strengths and

Figure 2.20 Self-Reflection Inventory

Read each statement and circle the numbers that are most like you.

1. I like new challenges.
2. I like to work with my friends.
3. I like to follow directions.
4. I like to examine things that interest me.
5. I like creating and discovering.
6. I like group work in class.
7. I like routines each day.
8. I like to understand how things work.
9. I like new things and ideas.
10. I like everyone to feel good.
11. I like to finish a job or assignment.
12. I like to think and solve problems.
13. I like to use my imagination and create things.
14. I like helping other people.
15. I like to see models and make things.
16. I like to read to get the information I need.
17. I like moving about.
18. I like everyone to do well and be happy.
19. I like to do things I feel comfortable with and are familiar.
20. I like to organize things so they make sense to me.
21. I like music and art.
22. I try to understand how others feel.
23. I like to follow patterns.
24. I like to see the details and parts.
25. I like to think about where new information can lead me.
26. I like to share ideas and problems.
27. I like to solve problems step by step.
28. I like to work with ideas, new models, and projects.

Circle the numbers below that you circled above.

A. 1, 5, 9, 13, 17, 21, 25 _____ total circled
B. 2, 6, 10, 14, 18, 22, 26 _____ total circled
C. 3, 7, 11, 15, 19, 23, 27 _____ total circled
D. 4, 8, 12, 16, 20, 24, 28 _____ total circled

If you had a higher total in A: You are more beach ball like.
If you had a higher total in B: You are more puppy like.
If you had a higher total in C: You are more clipboard like.
If you had a higher total in D: You are more microscope like.

encouraged her to go farther. She read well and wrote with imagination and flair. As she moved up in the grades, the freedom to be her self was curtailed. She could no longer use her creativity and fresh ideas to enhance her learning. She was forced to follow directions and observe limits (which were good skills for life), but with only that "modus operandi" and somewhat boring routine she became a "reticent consumer" as she moved

Figure 2.21   Beach Balls Learning Style

Concrete Random, Accommodator, Orange, Dynamic, Self-Expressive Learners, NF	
Innate abilities	**Work best when they**
Experimentation and discovery Risk taking and possibility thinking Adventurous and discovery oriented Intuitive and insightful Creative and independent Spontaneous and curious	Get to make choices Are self-directed Are in competition Can experiment through trial and error Can use brainstorming and have open-ended options Have activities that are hands-on They can create and use their imagination
Challenges	**To work on**
Having lockstep directions and limitations Making choices even if they like them Having no options or variety Working in a constant environment Always doing the same written task	Managing time and process Completing and follow through Delegating responsibility Being realistic about outcomes Accepting others' ideas Setting limits, being realistic

Instructional strategies: Brainstorming, problem solving, games, experiments, simulations
Activities they prefer: Considering, organizing, reorganizing, exploring, forecasting, processing, predicting, creating, recommending
Products: Editorials, problem solutions, games, simulations, inventions, experiments
Multiple intelligence strengths: Visual/spatial, musical/rhythmic, bodily/kinesthetic

through middle and high schools. She did not have opportunities to experiment, be spontaneous, and make choices as Figure 2.21 shows that a beach ball learning style prefers.

Puppy Learners

Jodie, my first daughter, was much more a puppy learner (truer to a firstborn). She was very much interested in people and her interactions with them. She was sensitive and highly emotional in her interactions with others. She was upset when others were upset and showed joy in other's happiness. She aimed to please. She liked recognition and needed feedback and positive affirmation that she was doing "whatever" well and according to expectations. She was intuitive and sensitive and had great empathy for her family and friends. She loved working with others and was often the mediator and consensus builder during conflicts (her own and others'). Figure 2.22 shows us the attributes of the puppy learning style.

Figure 2.22   Puppies Learning Style

Abstract Random, Diverger, Blue, Imaginative, Interpersonal Learner, SF	
Innate abilities	**Work best when they**
Empathic and intuitive Subjective, abstract, affective Read between the lines See the gestalt (forest) Personalize information Sensitive, flexible, and amenable Use imagination in their work	Have opportunities to work with others Have time for self-reflection Can connect with teacher and other learners Are given a rationale for learning Receive personal attention and support Work in a noncompetitive environment Engage in open communication
Challenges	**To work on**
Being detail oriented and exacting Working alone or following detailed directions Working with time limits and parameters Being corrected or receiving negative feedback Memorizing Working with difficult people Using lists and agendas Doing one task at a time	Picking a plan and sticking to it Focusing on time limits Giving attention to detail and precision Controlling impulsivity Controlling emotions Seeing details Including details in decision making

Instructional strategies: Cooperative group learning, webbing, mapping, media, personalized learning, role playing, music
Activities they prefer: Connecting, relating, expressing, sharing, presenting, interpreting, performing, counseling, imagining, peer interaction, dialogue, and discussion
Products: Creative arts, interview, journal
Multiple intelligences strengths: Interpersonal, verbal/linguistic

Microscope Learners

Pat, my microscope learner, was a diligent student. He was eager to learn and would research extensively on a topic to make sure the information was accurate and up to date. He liked to work alone at his own pace and delve as deeply as he wanted into the content. He wanted to know why we were doing what we were doing and what use it might be to him. He liked to get expert opinions and make his own conclusions about the information. He was highly competitive and wanted to be sure he was thorough and correct. He was often hard on himself and wanted accuracy and precision (not bad traits) to an extreme at times. He was easily frustrated if he didn't succeed to his level of satisfaction, and he was often intolerant of other students if they didn't measure up to his standards. See Figure 2.23 for the attributes of the microscope learning style.

Figure 2.23 Microscopes Learning Style

Abstract Sequential, Assimilator, Green, Analytical, Understanding, NT

Innate abilities	**Work best when they**
Valuing information and details	Have expert references and sources
Organizing and debating ideas	Feel confident and comfortable
Honing in on main points	Are working alone
Critical thinking	Have time for thorough investigation
Researching information	Can write analytically
Focusing on solutions and finding answers	Learn from lecture and reading
Examining details and forming theories	Can think in abstract terms and language
Working to success and recognition	
Analyzing theories and information	
Thorough logical learners	
Delaying gratification	
Challenges	**To work on**
Working with others in group discussions	Letting go of perfection
Hypothetical situations and simulations	Overobsession with grades
Building or creating projects	Being less critical and nonjudging
Expressing their emotions	Trying new things
Creative writing	Listening to others' ideas and suggestions
Open-ended situations or problems	Being aware of feelings
	"Lightening up"

Instructional strategies: Lecture, mastery, text, Internet & library resources, investigating problems, independent study.
Activities they prefer: Analyzing, reporting, speculating, inferring, hypothesizing, verifying, critiquing, outlining
Products: Reports, debates, presentations, research, theory development, lecture
Multiple intelligence strengths: Logical/mathematical, naturalist, intrapersonal

---

Clipboard Learners

Dayna was my clipboard learner. She wanted order and structure to the learning. She was first to ask these kinds of questions:

- What am I supposed to do?
- When is it due?
- Is there a rubric or scoring scale?
- Do I work alone or with a partner?
- How big should the report be?

She was a taskmaster for herself and for her group. She met deadlines and followed directions astutely. She was most often reliable and responsible. Others could always count on her to "get the job done." She would become anxious if things did not unfold according to plan, and she didn't deal

Figure 2.24 Clipboards Learning Style

Concrete Sequential, Converger, Gold, Common Sense, Mastery, ST	
Innate abilities	**Work best when they**
Precision and accuracy Planning and organizing Structured conditions and environment Striving for perfection Practicality, usefulness Details and specificity Precision and accuracy Compliancy with rules and standards Externally motivated Delay gratification	Have real experiences Are given concrete examples, not theories Have a structured, orderly, quiet environment Have procedures, routines, predictable situations Are given detailed directions and models Can see practical, hands-on applications Work in consistent and efficient surroundings Have guided practice for successful results
Challenges	**To work at**
Working without monitoring and feedback Selecting from choices Having random options Working without parameters and directions Hearing opposing viewpoints Being in new situations or trying new approaches Understanding others' feelings Using their imagination	Expressing their feelings Honoring process and product Honoring other learner styles Patience vs. immediate conclusions Listening to others Having reasonable expectations Seeing value in people as well as product Seeing the big picture

Instructional strategies: Structure and details in directions; hands-on approaches; how-to projects; computer learning; realistic, practical situations
Activities they prefer: Sorting, labeling, listing, collecting, charting, making, constructing, classifying, measuring, preparing, building
Products: Graphs, models, exhibits, timelines, dioramas
Multiple intelligence strengths: Logical/mathematical, naturalist, visual/spatial, bodily/kinesthetic

well with change or spontaneity. She was uncomfortable with ambiguity and choice and didn't like any surprises or deviations from the standards, routines, and rules. See Figure 2.24 for the attributes of the clipboard learning style.

LEARNING STYLES IN THE DIFFERENTIATED CLASSROOM

Literacy Learning

Literacy is one of the key focuses in classrooms everywhere, and it is important to recognize learning style preferences in reading, writing, speaking, and listening. Figure 2.25 shows those preferences for beach ball, puppy, clipboard, and microscope learning styles.

Figure 2.25   Learning Styles and Their Preferences for Reading, Writing, Speaking, and Listening

Styles	Reading Preferences	Writing Preferences	Speaking and Listening
Beach Ball **Abstract Random** Self-expressive	Likes variety of reading materials Needs a "hook" to focus Sees the big picture Imagination and fiction Science fiction Adventure Interesting reading Poetic and creative	Metaphors Imagination and fiction, including science fiction and fantasy Self-expression and personal Opportunities to use imagination and symbolism Variety and choice are important	Spontaneous conversation about things that intrigue Opportunities to listen to interesting ideas from others Brainstorming Using creative and metaphorical language
Puppy **Concrete Random** Interpersonal	Likes stories that have personal feelings and interesting people Biographies Likes to relate reading to their own lives Enjoys discussions and interpretations of reading Likes peer- and buddy-guided reading	Enjoys interviews Letter writing Collaborative writing Personal feedback Enjoys sharing personal feelings and those of others	Conversations about feelings and emotions Discussions about people Listening to others' ideas, thoughts, and feelings Think, Pair, Share
Clipboard **Concrete Sequential** Logical	Personal engagement Likes to read for practical reasons and information. How to . . . Prefers reality Likes guided reading with teacher direction Responds to reading to find out information	Likes to write to report or organize information Likes to write for practical purposes Interested in real-life situations Appreciates guidelines and models, examples and organizers	Likes to ask and answer questions about specific information and ideas Likes to listen to details
Microscope **Abstract Sequential** Analytical	Independent reading on topic of interest Likes details and description Likes challenges and intrigue in books Likes graphs, charts, lists Likes to process and question reading Reads for information	Essays Analytical pieces that require logic and are supported with research and evidence Likes detail and description in writing Likes to create rationales and use/find support evidence	Needs encouragement to engage in dialogue Appreciates deeper discussions that analyze ideas and clarify thinking

SOURCE: Reprinted from *Differentiated Literacy Strategies for Student Growth and Achievement in Grades K–6* by Gayle H. Gregory and Lin Kuzmich. Thousand Oaks, CA: © 2005 by Corwin Press. All rights reserved. www.corwinpress.com

Sing About Style

To help students recognize, remember, and appreciate the diversity of learners and learning styles in their classroom, the following song may be sung to the tune of "Clementine."

The Learning Styles Song (tune of "Clementine")

There are clipboards, there are clipboards, there are clipboards
In my class
They are practical and realistic
They like organizing facts
They follow directions, make a plan, like to finish a great job
They set a goal and make it happen. Clipboards like to get things done
They are helpful, they are helpful, they are helpful
In my class
I can ask them how to do things, keeping time while
Doing tasks.

There are puppies, there are puppies, there are puppies,
In my class
They like people and they're equal
To helping everyone do well
They work with others, listen carefully, and care about each one
They like to share all their ideas. Puppies like most everyone
They are helpful, they are helpful, they are helpful,
In my class
Puppies care and they are friendly and they listen
When I ask.

There are microscopes, there are microscopes, there are microscopes,
In my class
They like to read and do some research
Making sure about their facts
They're analytical and they're careful for they want to be so sure
That what you say is very truthful and the information is secure
They are helpful, they are helpful, they are helpful,
In my class
If I want logic and reason, microscopes will be right there.

There are beach balls, there are beach balls, there are beach balls,
In my class

They like moving and improving
What could be a boring task
They're creative, down to business, innovative, and hands on
They like a challenge, full of options, filled with energy and fun
They are helpful, they are helpful, they are helpful,
In my class
Beach balls look for possibilities, and variety
In the task

Student Journaling and Self-Reflection

Asking students to use a journal to reflect on a task or learning experience can help them be more conscious of their learning styles and more in control of their learning. Some journal prompts may include the following:

- Today I really liked it when . . .
- It was hard for me to . . .
- I really would rather . . .
- If I could make one request . . .
- If I could change one thing for tomorrow . . .
- If I do this again I would . . .
- I would need some help with . . .

Figure 2.26 offers a 3-R's journaling guide for students to use to reflect on and project their learning needs.

Figure 2.26   3 R's Reflection Journal

Really like . . .	Would rather . . .	Request . . .

DIFFERENTIATING INSTRUCTION FOR DIFFERENT LEARNING STYLES

We want students to be aware of their own learning and to be conscious of what they need to continue to grow. But it is also important for teachers to reflect on their instructional practices to ensure that they are providing learning opportunities that appeal to all learning styles and multiple intelligences.

Lesson Planning

Teachers can create their own tools for reflection on their instructional practice or they can use the checklist shown in Figure 2.27. This checklist will increase the chances that your units and lessons will appeal to the full range of diversity in your classroom and will help all your learners succeed.

Learner preferences for the four learning styles generally cluster as follows:

- *Beach balls.* Beach balls respond to choice and options for experimentation and creativity. But we also must recognize that these learners need deadlines, guidelines, and boundaries or else they may have trouble focusing or completing assignments. Balancing their creativity and spontaneity with time management and "stick to it" skills can be very important for beach balls.

- *Clipboards.* Clipboards like to have order, structure, and routine with clear guidelines and expectations. But life is not always predictable and organized. The unexpected occurs and then what? Clipboards need to break out of the routine and learn to deal with ambiguity, spontaneity, and anomalies. Dealing with the unexpected is also a life skill.

- *Microscopes.* Microscopes are more in-depth learners who like to analyze and investigate the "truth" they seek. They need sufficient time to go as deeply as they need for their learning while also recognizing that sometimes they have to move on. They also need help in working with others, developing collaborative skills, and seeing other people's points of view.

- *Puppies.* Puppies are generally collaborative learners and enjoy partner and group work, yet they also need to develop independent skills and to take risks and learn to trust their own judgment and work alone in new areas.

Figure 2.28 shows what a sample lesson on the Great Depression might look like differentiated for the four learning styles.

Figure 2.27   Lesson Planning Checklist: Have You Done Your Best to Know Every Learner in Your Classroom?

Considering Clipboards

☐ Clear directions and expectations
☐ Orderly, consistent, and efficient environment
☐ Timeline of assignments and the grading guidelines shared clearly and accurately
☐ Materials available, models or samples shown
☐ Real experiences, genuine need established
☐ Concrete examples, not theories
☐ Structured, orderly, quiet environment
☐ Procedures, routines, predictable situations
☐ Practical hands-on applications
☐ Guided practice for successful results

Considering Beach Balls

☐ Have a chance to make choices
☐ Are able to be self-directed at some time
☐ Are in a competitive situation on occasion
☐ Are allowed to experiment through trial and error
☐ Get a chance to brainstorm and deal with open-ended options
☐ Have activities that are hands on
☐ Are encouraged to create and use their imagination

Considering Puppies

☐ Opportunities to work with others
☐ Time for self-reflection
☐ Feedback, connect with teacher and other learners
☐ Have a rationale for the learning
☐ Must feel included and get some personal attention and support
☐ Environment is safe to take risks and mostly noncompetitive
☐ Open communication exists, their ideas are accepted

Considering Microscopes

☐ Have expert and ample references and sources
☐ Feel confident and comfortable
☐ Can work alone for part of the time
☐ Have time for thorough investigation
☐ Can write analytically
☐ Can learn from lecture and reading
☐ Can think in abstract terms and language
☐ Get a chance to delve into interest areas important to them

Figure 2.28   Sample Differentiated Lesson on the Great Depression

For the beach balls: Do something interesting with the content. Create a role play to depict the political situation during the depression, the social ramifications of the depression, and some of the events to remember. Create a visual to show how people lived during the depression. 	For the puppies: Help them connect with the personal aspects of the topic. How do you think people felt during the depression? What was done to raise the spirits of those who were struggling? Interview three or four people who lived through the depression. Prepare at least 10 questions at a variety of levels for the interview. 
For the clipboards: Provide concrete information. Describe the political and social situation during the depression. What were the contributing factors? List them in rank order from your perspective. Have a rationale for your ranking. 	For the microscopes: Help them connect with the deeper meanings of the topic. What was life like for people during the depression? Why did this era occur? How might it have been avoided? If it would happen today how would people react or spend their time?

NINE STRATEGIES FOR DIFFERENTIATING INSTRUCTION FOR LEARNING STYLES

1. Rationalize the learning as desirable skills or knowledge that is needed

Why? Give students a reason for learning. Connect to their world. The dinner conversation is often "What did you learn in school today?" and some students don't know. They have not had the luxury of being let in on the goals the teacher has targeted for their learning. Common sense and mastery learners want to know the direction they are going and why they might want to go there.

2. Provide opportunities for accessing information from a variety of accurate sources

Provide models and concepts and time to explore. What? The substance and content are clearly exposed, shared, and examined. Technology, resource materials, and other hands-on activities help create understanding and memorable learning.

3. Provide time for application and rehearsal

Practice with and find practical uses for the skill or knowledge. How does this work? So what? Experimentation and application in practical ways is necessary for all learners and also provides rehearsal for long-term memory retention.

4. Offer chances for creativity for dynamic interaction with the material and skills

What if? Students select opportunities to transfer the new learning to new situations. Will there be chances for application and creativity, not just "test regurgitation"? Well-structured, monitored, useful, meaningful, and creative projects, presentations, role plays, and exhibitions let that clipboard and microscope have structure and parameters yet allow the puppies and beach balls to interact and create.

5. Offer a flexible classroom

A classroom that has only desks in rows will not satisfy all learning styles. The ability to move furniture, set up centers or stations, and provide flexible groupings or partner work will be an asset to the diverse learners you teach. Quiet centers with headphones to block out noise for those learners who are easily distracted or, conversely, headsets to provide calming background music for reading will be a welcome addition to the room. Resources, materials, and technology will enrich and provide choice and freedom of access to all learners.

6. Know your learners and provide variety

Teachers who make a conscious effort to get to know their learners are always farther ahead in engaging and satisfying the diversity in the classroom. We use old adages that help us remember this. Some use a carpenters' analogy and suggest that we should "sand with the grain." Some suggest that it is easier to "go with the flow." A teacher from Montana offered that "it's easier to ride the horse in the direction it's already going."

7. Work with other teachers

It is so much more comforting (important for puppy-like teachers) to work with colleagues when you are trying something new. Planning lessons and units of study with learning styles in mind can be more fun and less stressful with a grade group team or a department teaching partner. The teachers' learning styles vary and bring different ideas to the planning table. We often teach as we learn best, so with a variety of teachers, more diverse learning strategies are considered and built into the lessons.

8. Build in reflection for students and yourself

Build on strengths but also challenge students to stretch in their styles. The more overt we are about learning styles and the diversity of individuals in the classroom, ideally, the more students will value that. They also need a chance to examine their actions and set goals for themselves. They should be able to recognize their strengths and preferences but also begin to consciously develop underused areas in their profile. For example, beach balls are often full of "neat" ideas but may need some help in working in time and task constraints. Learning style is not an excuse for a learner to abdicate the responsibility for areas where he or she is not strong but, rather, a consciousness-raising opportunity to continue to grow and also become more tolerant of others' styles. Logs, journals, "tickets out" (slips of paper that students fill in reflecting on their learning or performance; they provide feedback and are a communication/assessment tool for teachers), and classroom discussion can help.

9. Build the curriculum

Teachers can build their curriculum with a variety of learning strategies and assessment tools that accommodate all learners.

Figure 2.29   Reflections on Becoming: Looking Back, Looking Ahead

- What strategies in this chapter could you use?

- What can you do to help students identify their strengths and set goals?

- What strategies from this chapter would be helpful in gathering data about your students?

- What type of record keeping will you or your students use?

- What can you do immediately to attend to your students' learning styles?

Intelligences: 3
IQ or Many?

What is intelligence? What role does intelligence play in growth? Many theorists postulate answers for us about intelligence.

TWELVE INTELLIGENT BEHAVIORS

Art Costa and Bena Kallick (2000) propose that being intelligent means being able to handle the unexpected or the unknown with confidence and with strategies to problem solve. Costa and Kallick propose 12 intelligent behaviors that evolved into 16 Habits of Mind that help us with our thinking:

1. **Persistence:** to persist in spite of obstacles or challenges to find solutions to dilemmas or problems

2. **Managing impulsivity:** to control physical and emotional responses so that successful thinking can take place

3. **Listening with understanding and empathy:** to feel empathy for another by taking on his or her persona and experiencing the thoughts and feelings that that person might be having

4. **Flexibility in thinking:** to be able to adjust to, try, and explore other points of view

5. **Thinking about thinking (metacognition):** to be aware of one's own thinking and reflect on situations, challenges, or problems

6. **Striving for accuracy:** to focus on what quality looks like and to work toward quality, including correctness and clarity

7. **Questioning and posing problems:** to continue to be inquisitive and question new information to extend one's learning

8. **Drawing on past experience and applying it to new situations:** to reflect on past situations so that prior experiences are helpful in new situations

Figure 3.1   Sample Visual Organizer for Intelligent Behaviors or Habits of Mind

Behavior: Accuracy

Looks like:

Checking data from a variety of sources. Using dictionaries, encyclopedia, Internet, textbook, etc.

Sounds like:

I'd better check the spelling. The Internet might have something more up to date. Let's check that.

Feels like:

Pride in a task
Sense of control
Accomplishment

NOTE: See Figures 3.26 and 3.27 for visual organizers for the intelligent behavior or Habits or Mind persistence.

9. **Thinking and communicating with clarity and precision:** to use specific descriptive language that accurately conveys meaning

10. **Gathering data through all senses:** to fully understand new things and information by exploring one's environment using all the senses

11. **Creating, imagining, innovating:** to create something new, novel, or original by taking one's knowledge and skills and exploring solutions to problems

12. **Feeling wonderment and awe:** to be open, to feel confidence and passionate about thinking and learning and to be intrigued with the world and its wonder

13. **Risking:** to stretch oneself beyond ones comfort zone

14. **Using humor:** to laugh with others and at oneself

15. **Thinking collaboratively:** to be interdependent and reciprocal with others

16. **Open to possibilities for learning:** to be open, curious, humble, and proud about one's learning

Some teachers share these behaviors or Habits of Mind with their students and refer to a particular behavior as students are working on an assignment or project. Identifying what the behavior looks like, sounds like, and feels like may be useful to help students understand the behavior and to give them language that supports it. For example, if accuracy is the behavior

Figure 3.2 Habits of Mind and Thinking Styles

Beach Balls	**Puppies**
Being open to possibilities for learning Using humor Risking Flexibility in thinking Questioning and posing problems Drawing on past experience and applying it to new situations Creating, imagining, innovating 	Listening with understanding and empathy Gathering data through all the senses Thinking collaboratively Managing impulsivity
Clipboards	**Microscopes**
Striving for accuracy Questioning and posing problems Drawing on past experience and applying it to new situations Thinking and communicating with clarity and precision Managing impulsivity 	Persisting Thinking about thinking Striving for accuracy Thinking and communicating with clarity and precision

being discussed, creating a visual organizer like the one shown in Figure 3.1 might be helpful.

Each behavior, if mastered, can serve the individual well by enriching opportunities for thinking, problem solving, and human interaction. Certain behaviors might also be more evident in students with one learning style rather than another (see Figure 3.2 for the four learning styles and the suggestive predispositions of those learners to the intelligent behaviors) or Habits of Mind.) They may vary learner to learner, and the chart only suggests some that may be applicable. Our goal as teachers would be to identify these behaviors and help students develop all of them to the best of their ability.

EIGHT MULTIPLE INTELLIGENCES

Another way of looking at how we are smart is to examine Howard Gardner's Multiple Intelligences (1985). By no longer accepting the old

IQ score (Binet & Simon) as a sole indicator for intelligence, Gardner broadened how we look at intelligence. According to Gardner, intelligent people are able to do the following, using a variety of ways of accessing, processing, and applying information:

- Solve problems
- Handle crises
- Create things of value in a particular culture

Gardner believes that we have many resources in our "thinking toolkit" and that we can continue to increase those "tools" throughout life. We may have a predisposition for certain tools, but we can also grow more intelligent in our use of tools in all areas. Gardner's eight intelligences fall into several categories.

The two communication intelligences are verbal/linguistic and musical/ rhythmic.

   1. Verbal/linguistic: People with a high degree of this intelligence like to use words in different ways as a communication and thinking skill. They like to become involved in debates, storytelling, and poetry and enjoy the "lovely language" of metaphors, puns, analogies, and similes. They can read for hours and become lost in the language. They are often auditory learners and choose to listen, speak, read, and write. They love to communicate using a variety of tools such as letter, faxes, e-mails, and the like. Writers, actors, newscasters, and journalists generally have a high degree of this intelligence.

   2. Musical/rhythmic: People with a high degree of this intelligence have the ability to recognize and, often, to produce melody or rhythm and rhyme. They like music and are conscious of its impact. They appreciate and respond to a variety of music and rhythm sources. You often see these students beating out a rhythm that they pick up from their surroundings. They are highly responsive to many kinds of sounds. Musicians, song-writers, and vocalists have a high degree of this intelligence.

The next four intelligences relate to objects in our world.

   3. Visual/spatial: People with a high degree of this intelligence are very attuned to pictures, symbols, and drawings that appeal to the eye or the "mind's eye." They are able to see detail and appreciate graphs, charts, and representations to make sense of and develop an understanding of concepts and ideas. Artists, photographers, sculptors, and architects have perceptive powers of space and its relationships. These learners often think in pictures and have an innate sense of direction.

   4. Bodily/kinesthetic: People with a high degree of this intelligence have a keen sense of the tactile. They are aware of their own body and like to manipulate and handle materials to make sense of their world. They may excel in fine motor or gross motor skills from the neurosurgeon to the football quarterback or the Broadway actor. They like their learning to involve motion whether it be walking, building, or role-playing.

5. Logical/mathematical: People with a high degree of this intelligence are at home with numbers and reasoning. They are attuned to identifying patterns, recognizing cause and effect, and sequencing. They love to solve problems and pose and answer questions. They appreciate opportunities to analyze, assess, use spreadsheets, and organize information. Accountants, lawyers, and scientists are logically mathematical.

6. Naturalist: People with a high degree of this intelligence are very in touch with the natural world of animals and plants. This includes the geography of our world, landscape, and weather. These people prefer to be outdoors and are very astute about details in nature through pattern recognition, characteristics, and details. They use patterns and attributes to classify and organize. They have a deep appreciation for their environment.

The last two intelligences relate to the self.

7. Interpersonal: People with a high degree of this intelligence have a natural ability to interact with others. They are social beings who work well with others and are sensitive and intuitive to the feelings and moods of others. Often friendly and extroverted, they are attuned to the temperaments of those around them. They are appreciated in a team setting and are valuable members of the team.

8. Intrapersonal: People with a high degree of self-awareness are cognizant of and can manage their own emotions and feelings as well as use this knowledge to guide themselves. They value self-reflection and goal setting. They are aware of their strengths and needs and act on that information. They are able to hold up "the mirror" to see themselves clearly and respond to the reflection.

ASSESSING LEARNERS' MULTIPLE INTELLIGENCES

Teachers can use many different inventories and checklists to help students discover their strengths. This section provides a large variety to choose from.

The Most Like Me

Figure 3.3 offers an inventory that allows students to check off the statements that are most like them. They can count up the number in each section and transfer that number to the blocks in the graph. The numeric/color-coded summaries at the end can then be cut out to show their unique profiles.

Figure 3.3   The Most Like Me

Circle the numbers that are most like you.

1. You love to read.
2. You sing along with music when you learn some.
3. You love mysteries, puzzles, and games.
4. You like to go to new places and you do so easily.
5. You are well coordinated and move about easily.
6. You like collections and saving things.
7. You keep a diary or journal and write down your thoughts.
8. You know when someone is upset, angry, or depressed.
9. You like to tell and listen to jokes.
10. You'd like to play an instrument.
11. You like reading science fiction and about technological discoveries.
12. You notice other people's clothes and personal things.
13. You like to tinker with things and fix them.
14. You love being outdoors and enjoying the world.
15. You need quiet time by yourself.
16. You sometimes imagine how it would be to be someone else.
17. You just know when things sound right.
18. You turn on music when it's quiet.
19. You think it's fun to work with numbers and problems.
20. You can find your way around cities and buildings.
21. You often move your hands and body while you talk.
22. You like to listen to the birds singing and the crickets chirping.
23. You like to do things by yourself.
24. You like to belong to a club or a group.
25. You like words that are fun to say.
26. You like to sing, hum, whistle, or tap on the desk.
27. You like things organized in patterns and groups.
28. You are always doodling or drawing while thinking and listening.
29. You like games like charades and "hamming" it up.
30. You like to put things in categories and classify them.
31. You know what you like and what you are capable of.
32. You like to be with friends and just hang out.
33. You like to write stories and poems.
34. You get songs "stuck" in your head.
35. You like computers and working with them.
36. You enjoy TV, videos, and movies.
37. You have hobbies that let you build and make things.
38. You know a lot about animals and plants.
39. You like a challenge and set goals for yourself.
40. When you meet new people you are interested to learn about them.

Circle the numbers that are circled on the inventory.

Verbal/linguistic	1	9	17	25	33	Total ____ Green
Musical/rhythmic	2	10	18	26	34	Total ____ Red
Logical/mathematical	3	11	19	27	35	Total ____ Black
Visual/spatial	4	12	20	28	36	Total ____ Yellow
Bodily/kinesthetic	5	13	21	29	37	Total ____ Purple
Naturalist	6	14	22	30	38	Total ____ Orange
Intrapersonal	7	15	23	31	39	Total ____ White
Interpersonal	8	16	24	32	40	Total ____ Blue

Figure 3.4 How Are You Smart?

VERBAL/LINGUISTIC INTELLIGENCE	INTRAPERSONAL INTELLIGENCE
• I like to tell jokes, stories, or tales. • Books are important to me. • I like to read. • I often listen to radio, TV, tapes, or CDs. • I write easily and enjoy it. • I quote things I've read. • I like crosswords and word games.	• I know about my feelings, strengths, and weaknesses. • I like to learn more about myself. • I enjoy hobbies by myself. • I enjoy being alone sometimes. • I have confidence in myself. • I like to work alone. • I think about things and plan what to do next.
LOGICAL/MATHEMATICAL INTELLIGENCE • I solve math problems easily. • I enjoy math and using computers. • I like strategy games. • I wonder how things work. • I like using logic to solve problems. • I reason things out. • I like to use data in my work, to measure, calculate, and analyze.	**VISUAL/SPATIAL INTELLIGENCE** • I shut my eyes and see clear pictures. • I think in pictures. • I like color and interesting designs. • I can find my way around unfamiliar areas. • I draw and doodle. • I like books with pictures, maps, and charts. • I like videos, movies, and photographs.
INTERPERSONAL INTELLIGENCE • People ask me for advice. • I prefer team sports. • I have many close friends. • I like working in groups. • I'm comfortable in a crowd. • I have empathy for others. • I can figure out what people are feeling.	**BODILY/KINESTHETIC INTELLIGENCE** • I get uncomfortable when I sit too long. • I like to touch or be touched when talking. • I use my hands when speaking. • I like working with my hands on crafts/hobbies. • I touch things to learn more about them. • I think of myself as well coordinated. • I learn by doing rather than watching.
MUSICAL/RHYTHMIC INTELLIGENCE • I like to listen to musical selections. • I am sensitive to music and sounds. • I can remember tunes. • I listen to music when studying. • I enjoy singing. • I keep time to music. • I have a good sense of rhythm.	**NATURALIST** • I enjoy spending time in nature. • I like to classify things into categories. • I can hear animal and bird sounds clearly. • I see details when I look at plants, flowers, and trees. • I am happiest outdoors. • I like tending to plants and animals. • I know the names of trees, plants, birds, animals.

SOURCE: Reprinted from *Differentiated Instructional Strategies: One Size Doesn't Fit All*, by Gayle H. Gregory and Carolyn Chapman. Thousand Oaks, CA: Corwin Press © 2002. All rights reserved. www.corwinpress.com

How Are You Smart?

Figures 3.4 and 3.5 offer another inventory and profile students can use to identify their multiple intelligences. The students can compare their profiles with other classmates and work with partners who help "fill up" their toolkit by adding complementary strengths. Some teachers have students put the number of beads of each color according to the inventory on a shoelace, beading string, or elastic thread. Younger students may want to wear the necklace or bracelet to remind them of "how they are smart."

Figure 3.5   What Is Your Unique Multiple Intelligences Profile?

Word Smart							
Math Smart							
People Smart							
Music Smart							
Self Smart							
Picture Smart							
Body Smart							
Nature Smart							

SOURCE: Adapted by permission of Skylight Professional Development from page 57 of *Integrating Curricula With Multiple Intelligences: Teams, Themes, and Threads* by Robin Fogarty and Judy Stoehr. © 1995 IRI/Skylight Training and Publishing, Inc., www.skylightedu.com

NOTE: To read more about teaching with multiple intelligences profiles, see Fogarty and Stoehr (1995).

My Reflections

The My Reflections checklist (Figure 3.6) can be used with younger students. They can color the face that most closely agrees with their feelings about the activities on the left. If students are not yet reading, teachers may put pictures or symbols on the left to represent the activity.

Figure 3.6   My Reflections

Reading	☺	☻	☹
Writing	☺	☻	☹
Drawing	☺	☻	☹
Running	☺	☻	☹
Painting	☺	☻	☹
Singing	☺	☻	☹
Dancing	☺	☻	☹
Friends	☺	☻	☹
Animals	☺	☻	☹
Puzzles	☺	☻	☹

Figure 3.7   Graphing My Preferences: Student Sample

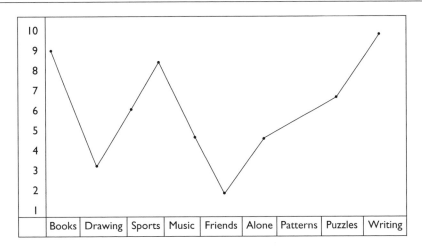

Graphing My Preferences

Students can be asked to rate their preferences for activities on a scale of 1 to 10 as shown for the sample activities named across the bottom of Figures 3.7 and 3.8. A dot can be placed beside the number above each activity, and the students can then connect the dots to show a graph. A blank template is provided (Figure 3.9) to allow this tool to be adapted for

Figure 3.8   Graphing My Preferences: Template 1

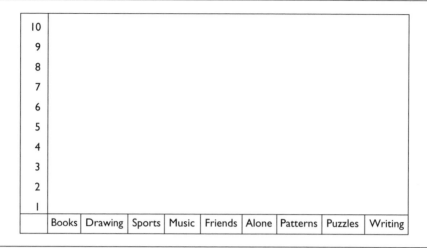

Figure 3.9   Graphing My Preferences: Template 2

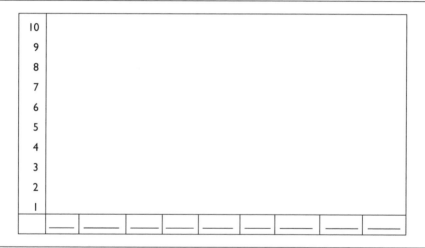

any other activities that relate to the areas of multiple intelligence—for example, the use of computers, building, acting things out, debating, singing, presentations, and so forth.

Cultivating Multiple Intelligences Every Day

Figure 3.10 gives a concise definition of each of the multiple intelligences, a slogan that fits that intelligence, and sample strategies and activities for that intelligence. Some teachers keep this chart with their plan books so that they have a reminder and numerous suggestions to use for each multiple intelligence.

Figure 3.10   Examining Multiple Intelligences

Definitions	Slogans	Cultivation of Intelligences
Verbal/Linguistic Uses language to read, write, and speak to communicate	Just say it!	• Play word games for vocabulary • Practice explaining ideas • Tell jokes and riddles • Play trivia games • Make up limericks
Musical/Rhythmic Communicates in rhyme and rhythm	Get with the beat!	• Interview people about their favorite music • Make up a song about your favorite things • Play name that tune • Create a class song • Share poems that are special to you
Logical/Mathematical Uses logic and reason to solve problem	Plot your course!	• Introduce graphic organizer to students and let them reflect on their use • Offer logic problems or situations and have students share problem-solving strategies
Visual/Spatial Ability to visualize in our mind's eye	Picture in your mind!	• Offer students opportunities to close their eyes and visualize: scenes, processes, and events • Allow and encourage students to add drawings and representations in their work or demonstrate understanding
Bodily/Kinesthetic Ability to learn and express oneself through the whole body	I do, I understand!	• Let students role-play processes and events • Create a dance or mime to illustrate an new learning • Create gestures or actions that demonstrate new learning
Naturalist Ability to recognize and classify	Mother Nature knows!	• Provide students with opportunities to classify and examine learning for like or different attributes • Allow students time for examination and a closer look
Intrapersonal Ability to be self-reflective	Looking back, looking ahead!	• Ask students to think about a plan for their assignment or to reflect on the process and set goals for improvement • Introduce journals or reflection time so students reflect on their work and their thinking
Interpersonal Ability to work with others	Together is better!	• Practice positive skills of active listening, encouragement • Show appreciation for the "smarts" of others

INSTRUCTIONAL PLANNING WITH MULTIPLE INTELLIGENCES

First things first! No matter what lens or framework one is using to plan, one first of all should begin with the end in mind. We must begin by identifying the standards that we expect students to accomplish in the lesson or unit of study. The concepts, big ideas, and skills are identified at the onset, and then activities may be planned to achieve those objectives.

Brainstorming Tools

If we are trying to build the multiple intelligences into a learning experience, we can begin with brainstorming possibilities in each of the intelligence areas.

Figure 3.11 suggests applications for all eight of the multiple intelligences that can be used in any content area, and Figure 3.12 offers a placemat organizer to encourage brainstorming in each multiple intelligence section. It is often useful to do this brainstorming with a group of teachers at the same grade level or who are teaching the same topic so that there is a diversity of thinking to generate multiple learning activities. We are all different and bring different strengths, perspectives, and preferences to the table, and that is advantageous because our students are so different and need many minds giving input and ideas for learning opportunities so that we might reach all learners.

Figure 3.11 Applying Multiple Intelligences

Gardner's Intelligences Described	Applications in Any Content Area
Verbal/Linguistic: Developing communication skills that include reading, writing, listening, speaking, and connecting information	Write Report Explain Describe and discuss Interview Label Give and follow directions
Musical/Rhythmic: Communicating and sensitivity to rhythm, rhyme, and music	Chant Sing Raps and songs Beat a rhythm Poetry Limericks Ballads

Gardner's Intelligences Described	Applications in Any Content Area
Logical/Mathematical: Organizing information through logic, abstract thinking, focusing on numbers, and patterns	Advance organizers Graphic organizers Puzzles Debates Critical thinking Graphs and charts Data and statistics
Visual/Spatial: Working with visualization and spatial relationships involving color, space, and media	Draw Create Visualize Paint Imagine Models Describe in detail
Bodily/Kinesthetic: Using the mind-body connections through movement and tactile and kinesthetic processes	Perform Create Construct Develop Manipulate Dance or mime
Naturalist: Being attuned to nature and recognizing the patterns and classification therein	Classify, sort Organize using criteria Investigate Analysis Identify, categorize
Intrapersonal: Independent work through self-direction, goal setting, and metacognition	Metacognition Logs and journals Independent study Goal setting Positive affirmations Autobiography Personal questions
Interpersonal: Cooperative work incorporating empathic social interaction	Group work Partner activities Reciprocal teaching Peer reading, editing, counseling Role play Class meetings Conferencing and sharing

Figure 3.12   Brainstorming Organizer for Multiple Intelligences Lesson Planning

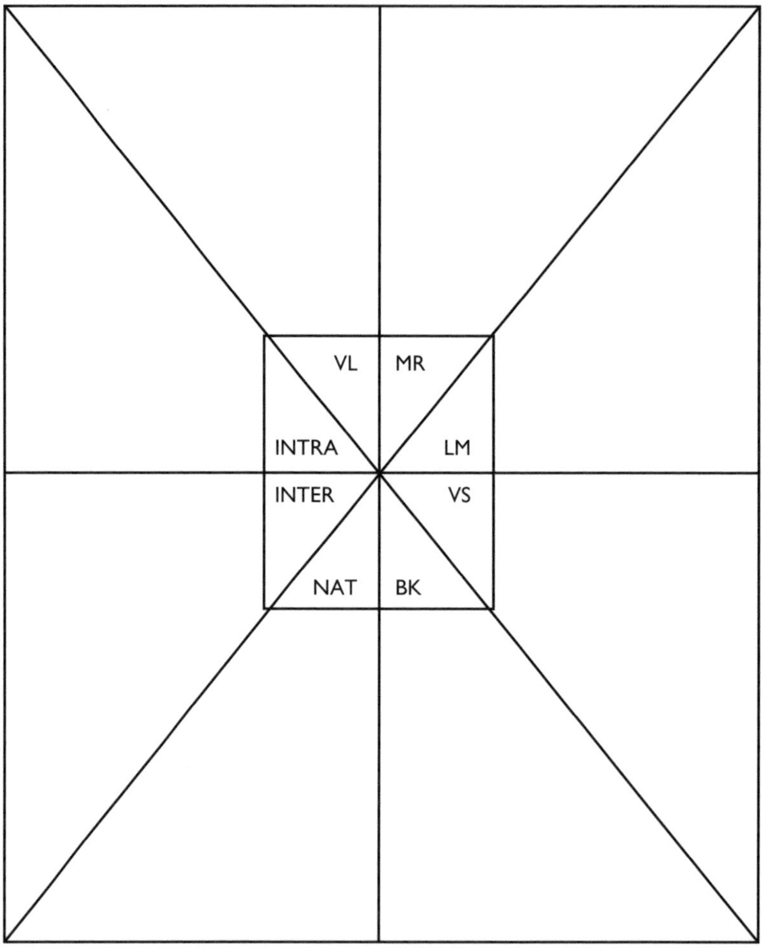

Content Area Strategies

Even though brainstorming takes place, it's not necessary to use all the ideas that have been generated. Teachers will be selective depending on the following:

- What their students need
- What might appeal to their students
- How much time they have to spend on the unit being planned

Of course, teachers will select the strategies with the most potential for learning and those with the highest possibility of engagement and attention by the students considering their strengths and needs. Figure 3.13 offers generic teaching strategies that can be used in the subject areas of social studies, science, language arts, and mathematics.

Figure 3.13   Subject Suggestions in Multiple Intelligences

	Social Studies	Science	Language Arts	Mathematics
Verbal/ Linguistic	**Identify** the pros and cons of . . .	**Explain** the function of . . .	**Retell** the story in your own words.	**Prepare** an editorial to suggest how math is useful in a variety of careers.
Musical/ Rhythmic	**Create** a song, poem, or rap to relate the events . . . Include appropriate background music during a presentation.	**Originate** a musical commercial for . . .	**Write** a poem or ballad that tells the story.	**Compose** a jingle to remember geometric shapes.
Visual/Spatial	**Draw** a cartoon or storyboard to show the events of . . .	**Diagram** the process of . . .	**Create** symbols for the characters in the story that show their characterization.	**Design** patterns with a variety of shapes to create an interesting artistic blanket.
Bodily/ Kinesthetic	**Act out** the . . . **Role-play** the . . .	**Mime** the process of . . . Create actions to show . . .	**Plan** a charade game to test your knowledge of the character, setting, and plot.	**Model** shapes or processes and have other students guess . . .
Logical/ Mathematical	Follow the directions to **develop a position** for a debate on . . .	**Predict** what would happen if . . .	**Construct** a logical argument for . . .	**Design** a cross-classification chart to show . . .
Naturalist	**Classify** the information for . . .	**Organize** the material into appropriate categories for . . .	**Analyze** the setting and how it contributes to the story.	**Categorize** and organize the processes.
Interpersonal	In a cooperative group, **build** a project that depicts . . .	**Conduct** an interview with a noted scientist who discovered . . .	**Describe** the relationships between the two main characters and why you believe this is so.	**Teach** others how you remember or use a formula.
Intrapersonal	In a journal **relate** a day in the life of . . .	Keep a personal diary to **show** what you know about . . .	**Decide** on the character that you would like to be friends with and tell **why?**	**Reflect on** what method is most useful to you in mathematics.

Choice Boards

Teachers may use a choice board to enable students to tap into areas of strength and comfort and also to prescribe opportunities to stretch in areas that need attention. Of course, clear outcomes or expectations must be considered when planning any instructional or rehearsal practice. The choice boards shown here offer a variety of generic activities (Figure 3.14), as well as sample lessons in literature (Figure 3.15) and American history (Figure 3.16). Another useful teaching strategy to use with the multiple intelligences in the content areas is cubing (see Chapter 4).

Figure 3.14   Choice Board for Multiple Intelligences

Verbal/Linguistic	Musical/Rhythmic	Visual/Spatial
Prepare a report	Create a rap, a song, or a ballad	Create a mural, a poster, or a drawing
Write a play or an essay	Write a jingle	Illustrate an event
Give directions for . . .	Write a poem	Draw a diagram
Create a poem or recitation	Select music to enhance a story or a event	Design a graphic organizer
Listen to a tape or view a video	Create rhymes that . . .	Use color to . . .
Retell in your own words		Create a comic strip to show . . .
Create a word web		Do a storyboard
		Create a collage with meaningful artifacts
Logical/Mathematical		**Bodily/Kinesthetic**
Create a pattern		Create a role play
Describe a sequence or a process	**Wild Card for Free Choice**	Construct a model or a representation
Develop a rationale		Develop a mine
Analyze a situation		Create a tableau for . . .
Create a sequel		Manipulate materials to . . .
Critically assess . . .		Work through a simulation
Classify, rank, or compare . . .		Create actions for . . .
Interpret evidence		
Design a game to show . . .		
Naturalist	**Interpersonal**	**Intrapersonal**
Discover or experiment	Work with a partner or a group	Think about and plan
Categorize materials or ideas	Discuss and come to conclusion	Write in a journal
Look for ideas from nature	Solve a problem together	Keep track of . . . and comment on . . .
Adapt materials to a new use	Survey or interview others	Review or visualize a way to . . .
Connect ideas to nature	Dialogue about a topic	Reflect on the character and express his or her feelings
Examine materials to make generalizations	Use cooperative groups to do a group project	Imagine how it would feel if you . . .
Label and classify	Project a character's point of view	
Draw conclusions based on information		
Predict . . .		

Figure 3.15   Sample Choice Board for Literature

Romeo and Juliet

Insert and act out a scene that you wrote for the play.	Create a photo essay or a brochure to chronicle the sequence of events in the play.	With a partner act out a scene from the play. You may videotape it if you wish.
Create a theme song or a rap with lyrics for *Romeo and Juliet.*	**Wild Card for Free Choice**	Design a map or paint/draw a picture of Verona.
Write a journal from Juliet's, Romeo's, or the nurse's perspective on the course of events.	Analyze the role of the monk. Was it in the best interests of the couple or was it part of something more sinister?	The dilemma: Did they have to die? What could have happened? Finish the story with a different ending.

Figure 3.16   Sample Choice Board for American History

American Presidents

Chronicle the journey that the president took to the White House.	Create a timeline of key events in his presidency.	Write a news release that captures the influences he had on world history.
Write a song or a ballad that tells his story as president.	**Wild Card for Free Choice**	What was the music of the period and how did it relate to historical events?
Create an interview with at least six questions that help get at the essence of his philosophy or intentions.	Brainstorm the key events in his presidency and create a mind map to show them.	Design a board game to show the events and critical events of the presidency.

TRIARCHIC INTELLIGENCE MODEL

Gardner's Multiple Intelligences theory and Robert Sternberg's Triarchic model (1996) work well together. Sternberg suggests that successful intelligence means being able to use knowledge with these intelligences:

- Practical intelligence
- Analytic intelligence
- Creative intelligence

Facts and information may be helpful by themselves on a quiz show, but to be truly valuable to a person, they must be used in an intelligent way. Sternberg suggests that successfully intelligent people have the following characteristics:

- Are naturally self-motivated, self-reliant, and independent
- Can control their impulses and are able to delay gratification
- Don't put off important things and do know when to persevere
- Begin, follow through, and complete obligations
- Are aware of their strengths and capitalize on them
- Will risk failure, take a chance, and accept blame if necessary
- Will persist to overcome difficulties
- Can see the big picture and the small parts
- Move beyond thought to action
- Can balance practical, analytical, and creative thinking

Practical Intelligence

This is the "so what" kind of intelligence that asks, "So what could we do with this?" This ability uses new information in a practical way. Action-oriented practical folks look to put new information to good use to solve problems and make decisions—street savvy and real-world application.

Analytic Intelligence

This intelligence analyzes new learning and uses it to solve problems, make choices, and judge critically. It includes the ability to pinpoint a problem, create options, offer solutions, gather resources, and manage their application. Educational testing sometimes focuses on this form of intelligence.

Creative Intelligence

The cognitive processes we use to create questions, problems, and projects that validate new learning make up creative intelligence. This frequently involves challenging existing assumptions and removing obstacles in our quest for new ways to do things. It is really like "thinking outside the box."

Lesson Planning With the Triarchic Model

Figure 3.17 shows phrases that can be used to design learning activities and assignments in each area of the triarchic model of intelligence. Figure 3.18 shows what a sample social studies unit on democracy might look like, and Figure 3.19 offers a blank planning template.

Thus we can challenge students not only to learn information but to use that information in practical, analytical, and creative ways. We can also facilitate these types of thinking through the use of Bloom's and others' taxonomies (see Figure 3.20), which we will discuss in greater detail in Chapter 4. Levels of analysis, application, synthesis, and evaluation move student thinking to the practical, analytical, and creative aspects, increasing the capacity for successful intelligence.

This approach will also engage different types of learners because of their learning styles or multiple intelligences. As you think about planning your next unit of study, consider how you might build in a practical, analytical, and creative approach to processing new information and refer back to Figure 3.19 for a planning template.

Figure 3.17   Phrases That Link Learning Activities to the Triarchic Model

Practical	Analytical	Creative
Show how . . .	Explain why . . .	Find a new way . . .
Demonstrate . . .	Show the parts of . . .	Use comic relief to show . . .
Based on your experience . . .	Identify the key aspects . . .	Take these materials . . .
Using your knowledge of . . .	Present step by step . . .	Explain a new way to . . .
Consider the problem . . .	Diagram how . . .	Connect . . .
		Become a . . .

Figure 3.18   Applying New Knowledge With the Triarchic Model: Sample Unit on Democracy

Unit or Topic: Democracy

Content: Attributes and values of democracy

Practical	Analytical	Creative
Apply knowledge in a **practical** way by creating a rationale to sell democracy to a new society.	**Analyze** the attributes of several other forms of government and compare and contrast them with democracy.	**Design** a new country and its government based on the principles of democracy.

Figure 3.19 Applying New Knowledge With the Triarchic Model: Planning Template

Unit or Topic:

Content:

Practical	Analytical	Creative

Figure 3.20 Applying New Knowledge With the Triarchic Model and Thinking Taxonomies

Unit or Topic:

Content:

Taxonomy	Practical	Analytical	Creative
Bloom (1956)	**Application** Adapt, transfer, solve, relate, transform, apply, employ, make, manipulate, use, transplant, convert, organize, model	**Analysis** Examine, dissect, inspect, sort, classify, separate, analyze, take apart, break down, scrutinize, discover, function, distinguish	**Synthesis** Build, regroup, blend, mix, compound, make, generate, join, combine, originate, develop, structure, imagine, predict, propose, improve, adapt, minimize, maximize, develop
Quellmalz (1985)	**Analysis** Parts to whole Relationships Cause and effect Sequencing	**Comparison** Similarities Differences Analogies Metaphors Synectics	**Inference** Predicting Hypothesizing Concluding Synthesizing Deducing Inferring
Williams (n.d.)	**Risk Taking** Try Dare Explore Predict Guess Experiment Estimate Adventure	**Complexity Management** Solve Improve Seek alternative Intricate Order Rank	**Elaborate** Expand Embellish Stretch Build Enlarge Add on Enrich

NOTE: For more information about the thinking taxonomies of Bloom (1956), Quellmalz (1985), and Williams (1989), see Chapter 4.

DIFFERENTIATING INSTRUCTIONAL STRATEGIES

Nine Research-Based Best Practices

The nine research-based best practices from *Classroom Instruction That Works* (Marzano, Pickering, & Pollock, 2001) give us clear guidelines about the strategies we need to use in all classrooms. These nine strategies have a proven impact on student learning as shown in the percentile gains in student achievement associated with each strategy (see Figure 3.21).

The application of these strategies has been researched across all grade levels and subject disciplines. They also align with how the brain works and with learning styles and multiple intelligences—that is, how different learners learn and process information. Figure 3.22 summarizes the nine strategies, linking them to percentile student gains, corresponding brain research, suggested tactics for the classroom, and the multiple intelligences that connect to them.

Figure 3.21   Nine Best Practices and Associated Percentile Gains in Student Achievement

Practice	Percentile Gain
Recognizing similarities and differences, using metaphors and analogies	45
Summarizing and note taking	37
Reinforcing effort and providing recognition	29
Assigning homework and practice	28
Generating nonlinguistic representations	27
Using cooperative learning	27
Setting objectives and providing feedback	23
Generating and testing hypotheses	23
Providing questions, cues, and advance organizers	22

SOURCE: Marzano, Pickering, and Pollock (2001).

NOTE: To read more about this topic, see Marzano, Norford, Paynter, Gaddy, and Pickering (2001).

Figure 3.22   Best Practices, Tactics, Styles, and Intelligences

Teaching Practice	% Gain	Connections to Brain Research	Tactics	Multiple Intelligences

Using similarities and differences, analogies, and metaphors	45	The brain is a pattern-seeking device. It naturally looks for connections and relationships between and among prior and new learning.	• Classifying
			• Compare/contrast
			  ➤ Venn
			  ➤ Synectics
			  ➤ Concept attainment
			  ➤ Concept formation
				Verbal/Linguistic
				Logical/Mathematical

(Continued)

Figure 3.22 (Continued)

Teaching Practice	% Gain	Connections to Brain Research	Tactics	Multiple Intelligences
Summarizing and note taking	34	Relevance and meaning are important to the brain. It deletes what is not useful.	• Mind maps • Concept webs • Jigsaw • Reciprocal • Templates and advance organizers	Logical/ Mathematical Verbal/Linguistic
Reinforcing effort and providing recognition	29	The brain responds positively to challenge and negatively to threat. Emotions enhance or negate learning.	• Goal setting and feedback/reflection • Journals • Portfolios	Verbal/Linguistic Interpersonal Intrapersonal
Assigning homework and practice	28	Practicing and rehearsal are necessary to put new information into long-term memory. Marzano suggests that learners need 24 practice trials to reach 80% mastery.	• Extension of application in interesting creative ways that stretch thinking	Logical/ Mathematical Could be any depending on the assignment
Generating nonlinguistic representations	27	The brain is a parallel processor. Visual stimuli are recalled with 90% accuracy.	• Mind maps • Graphic organizers • Models • Drawings • Charts	Logical/ Mathematical Visual/Spatial
Using cooperative learning	27	The brain is social and desires opportunities to process and make meaning through interaction and dialogue.	• Shared reading • Guided reading • Reciprocal learning • Peer editing • Buddy reading • Choral reading • Progressive writing • Jigsaw • Literature circles	Verbal/Linguistic Interpersonal
Setting objectives and providing feedback	23	Relaxed alertness is important for the brain. High challenge and low threat are optimal for learners. The brain likes to have purpose and know where the learner is going. This provides safety, clarity, and structure.	• Goal setting • Rubrics • Clear criteria • High expectations • Appropriate challenge and choice	Logical/ Mathematical Verbal/Linguistic
Generating and testing hypothesis	23	The brain is curious and seeks meaning and clarity. It establishes schemas for future use and makes meaning through patterns.	• Research papers • Investigations • Debates • Persuasive writing • Debates	Verbal/Linguistic Logical/ Mathematical
Providing questions, cues, and advance organizers	22	The brain appreciates wholes and parts. The brain has to have schemas and mental constructs on which to hook new learning.	• Levels of Bloom's taxonomy • Paul and Elder standards for questions • Agenda maps • Guided reading • Diagrams and charts • Graphic organizers • Templates and advance organizers	Verbal/Linguistic Logical/ Mathematical

NOTE: To read more about this topic, see Marzano, Norford, et al. (2001); Parry and Gregory (2003); and Gregory and Kuzmich (2005a, 2005b).

Five Natural Learning Systems

Barbara Given's five systems for natural learning incorporate emotional, social, cognitive, physical, and reflective learning systems (see Figure 1.1). These five systems can also be correlated with multiple intelligences to select instructional strategies based on learner needs and preferences (Figure 3.23).

Figure 3.23   Five Natural Learning Systems Correlated With Multiple Intelligences

System	Needs and Preferences	Multiple Intelligences
Emotional	• Positive climate • Emotional safety • Relevancy and meaning • Supportive learning community • Tapping into range of emotions	Intrapersonal Interpersonal Verbal/Linguistic
Social	• Inclusion • Respect • Enjoys others • Interaction • Interpersonal sharing • Authentic situations • Tolerance and diversity honored	Interpersonal Verbal/Linguistic
Cognitive	• Academic skill development • Prior and new learning connected • Seeks patterns, concepts, themes • Likes to see parts and the whole	Verbal/Linguistic Logical/Mathematical Visual/Spatial Bodily/Kinesthetic Naturalist Musical/Rhythmic
Physical	• Requires active involvement • Enjoys challenging tasks that encourage practice • Skills are a major part of this system	Bodily/Kinesthetic
Reflective	• Personal reflection on one's own learning styles • Reflects on successes, failures, changes needed • Metacognition of one's strengths and preferences	Intrapersonal

NOTE: To read more about the five natural learning systems, see Chapter 1.

Figure 3.24   Using TAPS: Total Group, Alone, Partners, or Small Groups

TOTAL GROUP Whole class instruction All students doing the same thing	Preassessment Presenting new information Modeling new skills Guest speaker Viewing a video Using a jigsaw strategy Guest speaker Textbook(s) assignment
ALONE All students working alone, may have a variety of tasks based on interest or readiness	Preassessment Journal entry Portfolio assessing Self-assessment Independent study Note taking and summarizing Reflection Tickets out
PARTNERS All students have a partner Random selection (card, color, etc.) Teacher selection Students choose a partner Task or interest oriented	Brainstorming Checking homework Checking for understanding Processing information Peer editing Peer evaluation Researching Interest in similar topic Planning for homework
SMALL GROUPS Homogeneous for skill development Heterogeneous for cooperative groups Random or structured by teacher or students Interest or task oriented	Problem solving Group projects Learning centers Cooperative group learning assignments Portfolio conferences Group investigation Carousel brainstorming Graffiti brainstorming

Interpersonal Intelligences

The TAPS organizer (see Figure 3.24) can be used to build in a variety of instructional strategies in a variety of class configurations: **T**otal group, **A**lone, **P**artners, and **S**mall groups. TAPS allows teachers to attend to multiple intelligences, learning preferences, and different levels of thinking.

Integrating Learning Styles and Multiple Intelligences

Silver, Strong, and Perini (2001) suggested integrating learning styles and multiple intelligences with learning experiences. Figure 3.25 offers an organizer using the puppy, microscope, clipboard, and beach ball learning styles.

Figure 3.25   Learning Activities Integrating Learning Styles and Multiple Intelligences

Topic:	Puppy	Microscope	Clipboard	Beach ball
Standards:				
Verbal/ Linguistic				
Musical/ Rhythmic				
Logical/ Mathematical				
Visual/Spatial				
Bodily/ Kinesthetic				
Naturalist				
Interpersonal				
Intrapersonal				

EMOTIONAL INTELLIGENCE

In his landmark book *Emotional Intelligence* (1995), Daniel Goleman suggests five domains of emotional intelligence based on the theory originating with Salovey (Salovey & Mayer, 1990; Salovey & Sluyter, 1997). This theory of emotional intelligence meshes nicely with Gardner's interpersonal and intrapersonal multiple intelligences. Goleman's five domains are as follows:

1. **Self-awareness:** The ability to appreciate one's own emotions

2. **Managing emotions:** The ability to manage and control emotions as a situation demands

3. **Motivation:** The ability to focus on the task despite obstacles and challenges

4. **Empathy:** The ability to be sensitive to and respond to the feelings and emotions of others

5. **Social arts:** The ability to manage and deal with others and their feelings and emotions

These domains can be recognized and nurtured by teachers in the classroom.

Self-Awareness

Self-awareness is the ability to appreciate one's own emotions. Self-aware people know they are experiencing a particular feeling and are able to label the feeling. They are able to recognize their emotions and seek support by articulating their feelings. They have a language of emotions and are in touch with their feelings without becoming engulfed. They have strategies to "change state" when they become aware of feelings they may want to change.

To help students become more aware of their emotions and feelings, teachers can encourage students to identify how they are feeling about a variety of things throughout the day, write about them, and share with others. The following prompts may be used in journaling or as exit slips. They can also be used as an inventory to help students think about the range of emotions. They can also empathize with historical and literary characters to identify their feelings in situations and analyze their reactions to those feelings.

Emotional prompts: Tell me a time when . . .

I get worried when . . .	If I'm worried, I . . .
I am happy when . . .	If I'm happy, I . . .

I get sad when . . .	If I'm sad, I . . .
I get confused when . . .	If I'm confused, I . . .
I get upset when . . .	If I'm upset, I . . .
I get nervous when . . .	If I'm nervous, I . . .
I get bored when . . .	If I'm bored, I . . .
I get excited when . . .	If I'm excited, I . . .
I get scared when . . .	If I'm scared, I . . .
I get angry when . . .	If I'm angry, I . . .

Managing Emotions

Managing emotions is the ability to manage and control emotions according to the demands of a given situation. Once one has recognized and named an emotion or feeling, the next step is to be able to manage the emotion or feeling. It is the skill of soothing, de-escalating, or curtailing as needed.

Teachers can help here by assisting students with strategies to defuse negative emotions as they occur in the classroom and, ideally, over time as students continue to practice strategies for managing emotions in their lives. To bring about a safe, supportive, nurturing classroom climate, teachers must help students feel confident that they are physically, emotionally, and psychologically safe in their environment. Teachers can help by using "teachable moments" to model problem solving and de-escalation when tempers or emotions flare. Having students understand about the fight-or-flight response and how the brain reacts to stress or fear can help them realize that they need time to "upshift" in the brain when their thinking has been "emotionally hijacked" by fear or stress.

Useful strategies for regaining composure include the following:

- Deep breathing
- Counting to 10 slowly (several times in some cases)
- Going for a walk
- Sitting quietly and becoming aware of feelings and how the body is reacting

All of these strategies can help students "downshift" and regain their thought processing and cognitive abilities. In less stressful times, students can view videos or discuss situations in stories or texts where people have become emotionally hijacked and then problem solve about how the situation could be handled.

Many situations in life that we read about or see everyday could perhaps have a more positive outcome if people had better strategies to manage stressful and fight-or-flight responses. We owe it to students to help them develop positive life skills that may be more useful to them in the long term than test scores.

Motivation

Motivation is the ability to focus on the task at hand despite obstacles and challenges. This domain is perhaps one that many of our students lack. It is the ability to "keep on truckin'" in the face of barriers and setbacks. Some in our society seem to have lost a work ethic to keep them self-motivated to hang in there until a task or project is finished. Some students need extrinsic rewards and do not like the uncomfortable feelings that may be evoked when the "going gets tough."

Flow

The notion of "delayed gratification" is not commonplace for some in our "feel good" society. Goleman (1995, 1998) suggests that it is closely related to "flow" (Csikszentmihalyi, 1991) or that "in-the-groove" feeling we get when things are going along and our challenge matches our skill level closely.

Csikszentmihalyi (1991) proposes seven conditions that are present when flow is experienced:

- Unaware of the passage of time
- Intrinsic motivation
- Ongoing feedback
- Action quickly follows inspiration
- Sense of control
- Unself-conscious
- Challenged at one's skill level

Persistence

When we consider Costa and Kallick's (2000) intelligent behaviors (Habits of Mind) we can see that several behaviors can help students with self-motivation—particularly persistence, precision, and accuracy. But students need support from teachers as well as strategies to "keep on keeping on" when they feel like quitting.

Teachers who are in tune with students can identify the need for basic skills such as persistence. Persistence is necessary to be able to keep a positive attitude when students are stumped or feeling overwhelmed with a difficult task. Teachers can talk about how persistence looks, feels, and sounds. They can create a T chart (Figure 3.26) or Y chart (Figure 3.27) to help students identify the behaviors associated with persistence.

Figure 3.26   Persistence T Chart

Persistence

Looks Like	Sounds Like
Keep working	I need some help, please.
Try other things	Any suggestions?
Get other resources	I think I'll try . . .
Think about any method	Maybe if I . . .
Brainstorm alternatives	I might be able to . . .
Ask a friend or a classroom	What did you do to . . . ?
Ask an adult	

Figure 3.27   Persistence Y Chart

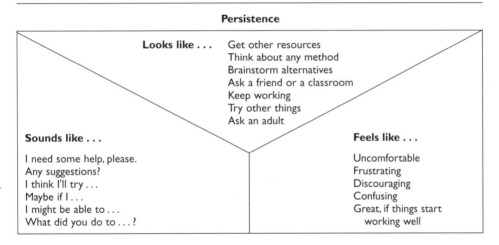

Persistence

Looks like . . .   Get other resources
Think about any method
Brainstorm alternatives
Ask a friend or a classroom
Keep working
Try other things
Ask an adult

Sounds like . . .

I need some help, please.
Any suggestions?
I think I'll try . . .
Maybe if I . . .
I might be able to . . .
What did you do to . . . ?

Feels like . . .

Uncomfortable
Frustrating
Discouraging
Confusing
Great, if things start
working well

Empathy

Empathy is the ability to be sensitive to and respond to the feelings of others. Empathy usually begins in early childhood as astute parents talk with children about feelings they are having, discuss feelings others are experiencing, and model appropriate responses. Empathy basically means to "feel with" another person, animal, or thing. Some people are highly evolved in their ability to empathize with others, actually "experiencing" others' emotions, but some people, unfortunately, are not.

As Robert Sylwester (2005) points out, "Empathy is an important trait in that it leads to the ethical and altruistic behavior necessary in effective conflict resolution" (p. 64).

Empathy is a skill that is lacking in those who are involved in crimes of violence where they are not able to "feel for another" and have no respect for another life whether human, animal, fish, or fowl. With a lack of empathy and an inability to self-regulate, some young people are a real threat to others and, ultimately, to themselves.

Many children learn empathy from positive adult role models in early childhood, but many learn the opposite in an environment void of respect for others' feelings or concern for others' suffering. Teachers are faced with the somewhat daunting task of helping students who have not had positive examples of empathy to learn to consider the feelings and safety of others in the classroom—hopefully, transferring that skill to their real lives outside the classroom and school. Teachers can use Figure 3.28 to focus on empathy as they discuss the feelings and emotions of fictional characters in a story, novel, or play or nonfictional characters in a historical or scientific unit.

Social Arts

The social arts cover the ability to manage and deal with others and their feelings and emotions. This domain involves using one's social skills appropriately to manage situations and emotions to a positive and constructive end. People with a high degree of social skill can do the following:

- Read body language well
- Anticipate others' needs
- Respond appropriately to others
- Soothe or reinforce others' behaviors in a positive way

People with a high degree of social skill are viewed as "social stars" and are generally popular and well liked. They have "people skills" and perform well in leadership positions because people respond to their caring ability to include others and make social interactions positive.

Teachers should, of course, model positive social skills that they hope students will emulate. However, unless social skills are labeled and taught, students may miss modeling that is too subtle. Basic skills—attentive listening, respecting others' space and possessions, using polite language—may seem too basic but may in fact be needed in many classes today. Again, these skills may be posted on T charts and Y charts as shown in Figures 3.26 and 3.27, referred to, and practiced in peer and small-group interactions. Teachers should never assume that students are aware of these skills and know how to behave appropriately.

WORKPLACE INTELLIGENCE

All this may seem like a tall order for teachers, but character education is built in to most state curricula, and when we look at the expectations of the

Figure 3.28 Empathy Chart

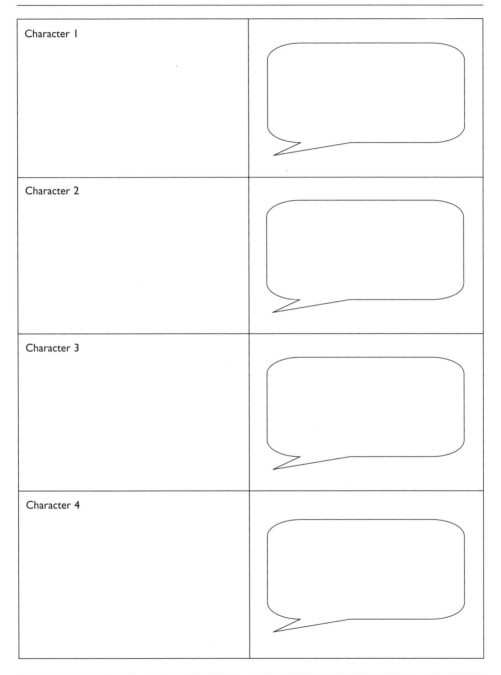

workplace and society in general, it behooves us as educators to get on board with the teaching of emotional intelligence. The SCANS (Secretary's Commission on Achieving Necessary Skills) report *What Work Requires of Schools* (U.S. Secretary of Labor, 1991) stresses personal qualities that include responsibility, self-esteem, sociability, self-management, and integrity/honesty:

- **Responsibility:** exerts a high level of effort and perseveres toward goal attainment
- **Self-esteem:** believes in own self-worth and maintains a positive view of self
- **Sociability:** demonstrates understanding, friendliness, adaptability, empathy, and politeness in group settings
- **Self-management:** assesses self accurately, sets personal goals, monitors progress, and exhibits self-control
- **Integrity/honesty:** chooses ethical courses of action

Daniel Goleman (1998) also reminds us that in an international survey of employers, data indicated that "emotional competencies were found to be twice as important in contributing to excellence as pure intellect and expertise" (p. 31).

SUMMARY

Our goal in education is not just "stuffing stuff" into short-term memory for a test. It is developing and nurturing the intelligence strengths of every learner, whatever those intelligences may be.

We are preparing students for their futures, not ours. Thus we must help them develop the tools they need to succeed. Helping them develop their intelligences and intelligent behaviors—multiple, triarchic, successful, emotional, and so forth—will better prepare them for successful futures.

Thinking Skills and Styles

<h1>4</h1>

A few years ago, I was presenting a session on thinking skills at a conference in San Francisco. I got into the hotel elevator laden down with materials on my way to the presentation room. A mother and daughter were also on the elevator. The mother asked if I was part of the education conference going on in the hotel. I said yes. She then asked my topic. I told her my session focused on integrating thinking skills across the curriculum. "Oh," she said and looked at her daughter. "You did some thinking last year at school, didn't you dear?" The little girl nodded with a questioning look on her face, and I smiled wondering to myself whether we are ever explicit enough about teaching thinking. Do we plan for it? Or does it just happen or not happen?

THINKING DEFINED

Thinking is a mental process that occurs when we solve problems and make decisions. Thinking is both a creative phase, wherein ideas are created anew (new to the learner), and a critical phase when ideas are evaluated or judged. These may be done independently or interdependently.

To become a better thinker, one needs to practice the skill just as one would practice any other new skill. Frequent practice sessions with a variety of content will enable students to develop the necessary skills, habits, and attitudes. Every standards-based curriculum across most nations includes skills in problem solving, decision making, critical thinking, and creative thinking. Ideally, if we are successful as educators we will have done more mind *building* than mind *stuffing*.

It has been said that thinking instruction will help with the following:

- Reading, writing, and listening
- Promotion of mental health
- Dealing with the negative effects of society

It also can enable students to be more successful in personal relationships, in careers, and in the world. The student benefits when he or she thinks creatively, makes decisions, solves problems, visualizes, knows how to learn, and reasons.

Creative Thinking

Creative thinking uses imagination freely, combines ideas or information in new ways, makes connections between seemingly unrelated ideas, and reshapes goals in ways that reveal new possibilities.

Decision Making

Decision making specifies goals and constraints, generates alternatives, considers risks, and evaluates and chooses best alternatives.

Problem Solving

Problem solving recognizes that a problem exists (i.e., there is a discrepancy between what is and what should or could be), identifies possible reasons for the discrepancy, and devises and implements a plan of action to resolve it. In problem solving, one also evaluates and monitors progress and revises plans as indicated by findings.

Seeing Things in the Mind's Eye

This refers to organizing and processing symbols, pictures, graphs, objects, or other information—for example, seeing a building from a blueprint, understanding a system's operation from schematics, grasping the flow of work activities from narrative descriptions, or knowing the taste of food from reading a recipe.

Knowing How to Learn

This refers to recognizing and using learning techniques to apply and adapt new knowledge and skills in both familiar and changing situations. It involves being aware of learning tools such as personal learning styles (visual, aural, etc.), formal learning strategies (note taking or clustering items that share some characteristics), and informal learning strategies (awareness of unidentified false assumptions that may lead to faulty conclusions).

Reasoning

Reasoning discovers a rule or principle underlying the relationship between two or more objects and applies it in solving a problem. For example, reasoning uses logic to draw conclusions from available information, extracts rules or principles from a set of objects or written text, applies rules and principles to a new situation, or determines which conclusions are correct when given a set of facts and a set of conclusions.

FREQUENTLY ASKED QUESTIONS ABOUT TEACHING THINKING

Can Thinking Be Taught?

There is sufficient research to show that both critical and creative thinking can be taught. This also includes creativity and originality.

Isn't It Only for the Gifted?

The definition of giftedness is often arbitrary. A student may be considered gifted as a result of testing and scores in giftedness. Or it may be that the student is deemed cooperative, works hard, and does above-average work. It may be that he or she is a "good memorizer" and gets great test scores. These characteristics do not necessarily indicate the potential to be a unique thinker.

Is It Really Important?

Thinking is an important part of all people's lives and is a part of everything they do. Choices, decisions, and problem solving all rest on the quality of thinking.

Is It Possible in All Subject Areas?

It is possible to be a critical and creative thinker in any curricular area. Examination and exploration of content—testing assumptions, making predictions, and detecting errors—can be done with most content in any discipline.

Does Thinking Just Happen With a Good Teacher?

Expert teachers tend to naturally go beyond the "sit and get" approach to the curriculum. This may enhance the learning, but without a conscious approach to building in thinking and attending to the different modes of thinking, it is only a haphazard experience. This method of letting thinking happen is more "by luck or by golly" than intentional.

Can Thinking and Content Be Integrated?

Some schools have designated a whole course in thinking, whereas other schools look at thinking across the curriculum. Each teacher makes a conscious effort to build in thinking activities in his or her discipline area. The faculty as a whole can develop a scope and sequence by grade level or course so that thinking is integrated horizontally and vertically in the curriculum.

How Can We Get Started?

A place to begin may be to start reading books about thinking skills and how they might be taught. Many teachers also begin by identifying the basic principles, concepts, and beliefs that students should know and understand. These are often referred to as the big ideas that we want students to carry on through life, not just the "trivial pursuit" of facts and dates that can be "spit back" on a test. As teachers revise the curriculum, they look for ways that students can wrestle with these big ideas, using processes for critical and creative thinking.

How Do Students React to Thinking?

Students may be surprised, confused, or both when they are asked to think in class—especially older students who have been passive receivers throughout most of their school careers. Many students respond with, "Just tell us what we should know," because thinking is hard work and requires active involvement. Often, teachers share the SCANS report with students (see below), which identifies the workplace skills that employers and people value, including the ability to think both creatively and critically.

WORKPLACE THINKING SKILLS

The SCANS report *What Work Requires of Schools* (U.S. Secretary of Labor, 1991) by the Secretary's Commission for Acquiring Necessary Skills listed five competencies that 21st-century workers need to compete in the global market:

1. Identification, organization, planning, and allocation of resources

2. Being able to work with others

3. Acquiring and using information

4. Understanding complex interrelationships

5. Working with a variety of technologies

Acquiring and Using Information

Within Skill Set 3, the SCANS report further itemizes workplace skills as follows:

- Acquires and evaluates information
- Organizes and maintains information
- Interprets and communicates information
- Uses computers to process information

BLOOM'S TAXONOMY OF CRITICAL THINKING

Benjamin Bloom and a group of other scholars were exploring educational objectives and recognized that learning involved both identification of content and the ways in which students interact with the content. Bloom (1956) focused his work on examining and classifying the behavior of students in relation to content, identifying six thinking levels:

1. **Knowledge:** learning information

2. **Comprehension:** understanding information

3. **Application:** using information

4. **Analysis:** examining parts

5. **Synthesis:** using information differently

6. **Evaluation:** judging information

The six levels are not necessarily hierarchical but attend to information in different ways. For example, knowledge and comprehension levels are more the brain's quest to acquire or access knowledge to construct meaning and understanding, whereas application, analysis, synthesis, and evaluation are ways of extending information.

Knowledge

- It is expected that the student will know the information and be able to restate it, but not necessarily use or apply it.

- Knowledge is not necessarily the simplest level in that the information may be quite complex, such as "the causes of the Iraqi war," or quite simple, as in "what is the capital of the country?"
- Knowledge is foundational; other levels can't be accomplished without the data to do so.
- Knowledge can be remembered in many ways: through memorization, mnemonics, embedded in rhyme or rhythm, illustrated in graphics or pictures.
- Parroting back knowledge does not necessarily mean deep learning.

Comprehension

- Students at the comprehension level are able to recall and use the information.
- Evidence of comprehension may come in several forms:

  Translation: restate or describe information in one's own words

  Interpretation: describe the key points and the connections

  Extrapolation: take information further to draw conclusions, consequences, implications, and/or predictions

Application

- Information should be used in a new context or setting.
- Information should be transferable when needed.
- As a natural outcome of their knowledge and comprehension, a student should initiate application and not be teacher directed.

Analysis

- This requires the student to look at the component parts of the information.
- A student should "read into" the information and note subtle inferences.
- This does not mean changing the meaning or message.

Synthesis

- This process requires putting the knowledge together in a new or novel way.
- It may seem a creative process, but it should be done critically to produce a creation, not just something new but something that shows planning and thought.
- The creation doesn't have to be unique in the universe, just unique to the student creating it.

Evaluation

- Opinion without criteria and rationale is not evaluation.
- Evaluation includes the following:

  Consideration of alternatives before making a judgment based on criteria developed by the student.

  Defending the choice with a rationale for selection.

INSTRUCTIONAL STRATEGIES USING BLOOM'S TAXONOMY

Figure 4.1 suggests verbs that can be used to direct student thinking at each level of Bloom's taxonomy, and Figure 4.2 does the same with action words. The action words offer enough variety so that visual, auditory, and kinesthetic learners can all find a level of comfort. The thinking levels also allow for right- and left-hemisphere dominance to find balance.

Figure 4.1   Directing Verbs for the Six Levels of Bloom's Taxonomy

Thinking Level	Definition	Directing Verbs
Knowledge Learn information	Recall the facts and remember previously learned information	Describe, list, identify, locate, and label
Comprehension Understand information	Understand the meaning of and the how and why of events	Explain, give examples, paraphrase, summarize
Application Use information	Transfer the skill or knowledge to another situation or setting. It tests knowledge and comprehension.	Infer, predict, deduce, adapt, modify, solve problems
Analysis Examine parts	Break down information to specific parts so that the whole can be understood. Understanding structure can help with comparisons.	Discriminate, classify, categorize, subdivide, delineate
Synthesis Use differently	Combine elements to create new and different ideas or models	Induce, create, compose, generalize, combine, rearrange, design, plan
Evaluation Judge the information	Rank or rate the value of information using a set of criteria	Judge, compare, criticize, contrast, justify, conclude

Figure 4.2   Action Words for the Six Levels of Bloom's Taxonomy

Level of Taxonomy	Action Words
Knowledge	Who, what, where, when, why, which, recall, locate, repeat, label, name, recite, find, relate, identify, select, find, show e.g., Name the mountain ranges on the West Coast.
Comprehension	Define, outline, reword, reconstruct, understand, calculate, conceive, paraphrase, transpose, convert, explain, interpret, demonstrate, draw, illustrate, summarize, translate e.g., Explain photosynthesis in your own words.
Application	Adapt, transfer, solve, relate, transform, apply, employ, manipulate, use, utilize, transplant, convert, organize, model, produce, make, diagram, debate e.g., Using _____ solve the following dilemma . . .
Analysis	Examine, dissect, inspect, sort, classify, separate, analyze, take apart, break down, scrutinize, discover, function, distinguish e.g., Inspect the menu at the local fast-food restaurant and identify the food groups available.
Synthesis	Build, regroup, blend, mix, compound, make, generate, join, combine, originate, develop, structure, imagine, predict, propose, improve, adapt, minimize, maximize, develop e.g., Rewrite the story of the "Three Little Fish" based on "The Three Little Pigs."
Evaluation	Judge, weigh, decide, rate, rank, grade, arbitrate, determine, assess, appraise, disprove, justify, support, estimate, interpret e.g., Justify your position about . . .

Wait Time and Quality Questioning

Wait time is crucial in a brain-friendly thinking classroom. We have known for years, thanks to educator Mary Budd Rowe (1986), that people need wait time so that the brain can access information stored in the unconscious long-term memory. It takes at least 3 to 5 seconds to retrieve often-used information, longer for information that has not been accessed for a while. Teachers who want quality thinking to take place need to allow for more than tenths of seconds before calling on a student for an answer to a question (Walsh & Sattes, 2005).

Think, Pair, Share (McTighe & Lyman, 1988) is a wonderful strategy to increase student thinking and build in wait time. Students "prime the pump" and open previously closed mental files during the *think* alone part of the strategy. Then they *pair* up with another student and *share* their thinking. Richer and fatter answers result, and generally, more students are thinking about the topic than playing the avoidance game during total class discussions.

By formulating and asking questions at different levels of the taxonomy, teachers can tap into all levels of thinking, posing questions that are challenging but not too difficult for diverse students. Figure 4.3 provides suggestions for question starters and potential activities at all six levels of the taxonomy. This chart can help teachers design projects, assignments, and center activities that engage a variety of levels of thinking and also appeal to the different multiple intelligences and learning styles.

Cubing

Cubing is another instructional technique that helps students look more closely at a topic through the lens of Bloom's taxonomy (Cowan & Cowan, 1980; Gregory & Chapman, 2002; Tomlinson, 2001).

The cube will have six sides:

- One side of the cube may say: Describe or tell about it.
- The second side: Compare it with something else.
- The third side: Associate it with another idea.
- The fourth side: Analyze it and tell the component parts or attributes.
- The fifth side: Apply it in another situation or to solve a problem.
- The sixth side: Argue for or against it based on criteria.

Cubes may vary with levels of thinking appropriate to the level of readiness of the student or group (see Figure 4.4). Cubes may also be constructed with tasks in a particular area of multiple intelligence such as visual/spatial, verbal/linguistic, bodily/kinesthetic, or intrapersonal.

Why Do We Use Cubes?

Cubing (with many sides) also allows students to look at an issue or topic from a variety of perspectives and to develop a multidimensional approach to considering a topic rather than a single one.

Cubes offer a chance to differentiate learning by readiness (familiarity with content or level of skill), student interest, and/or learning profile (multiple intelligences).

The cubes may vary in color and tasks depending on the abilities and interests of a small group (see Figure 4.5). They can add an element of novelty and fun to the learning by providing uniqueness to the lesson. It is a great strategy for tactile kinesthetic learners as well as visual and auditory learners whereby they reinforce concepts and expand and rehearse learning.

Figure 4.3 Question Starters and Classroom Activities Differentiated According to Bloom's Taxonomy

QUESTION STARTERS

Level I: KNOWLEDGE (Recall)

1. What is the definition for . . . ?
2. What happened after . . . ?
3. Recall the facts.
4. What were the characteristics of . . . ?
5. Which is true or false?
6. How many . . . ?
7. Who was the . . . ?
8. Tell in your own words.

Level II: COMPREHENSION

1. Why are these ideas similar?
2. In your own words retell the story of . . .
3. What do you think could happen?
4. How are these ideas different?
5. Explain what happened after.
6. What are some examples?
7. Can you provide a definition of . . . ?
8. Who was the key character?

Level III: APPLICATION (applying without understanding is not effective)

1. What is another instance of . . . ?
2. Demonstrate the way to . . .
3. Which one is most like . . . ?
4. What questions would you ask?
5. Which factors would you change?
6. Could this have happened in . . . ? Why or why not?
7. How would you organize these ideas?

POTENTIAL ACTIVITIES

1. Describe the . . .
2. Make a timeline of events.
3. Make a facts chart.
4. Write a list of . . . steps in . . . facts about . . .
5. List all the people in the story.
6. Make a chart showing . . .
7. Make an acrostic.
8. Recite a poem.

---

1. Cut out or draw pictures to show an . . .
2. Illustrate what you think the main idea was.
3. Make a cartoon strip showing the sequence of . . .
4. Write and perform a play based on the . . .
5. Compare this _____ with _____
6. Construct a model of . . .
7. Write a summary report of an event.
8. Prepare a flowchart to show the sequence . . .

---

1. Construct a model to demonstrate using it.
2. Make a diorama to illustrate one event.
3. Make a scrapbook about the study.
4. Design a relief map to include relevant information about an event.
5. Produce a collection of photographs to illustrate a particular aspect of the study.
6. Paint a mural expressing the theme.

QUESTION STARTERS

Level IV: ANALYSIS

1. What are the component parts of . . . ?
2. What steps are important in the process of . . . ?
3. If . . . then . . .
4. What other conclusions can you reach about . . . that have not been mentioned?
5. The difference between the fact and the hypothesis is . . .
6. The solution would be to . . .
7. What is the relationship between . . . and . . . ?

Level V: SYNTHESIS

1. Can you design a . . .
2. Why not compose a song about . . . ?
3. Why don't you devise your own way to . . . ?
4. Can you create new and unusual uses for . . . ?
5. Can you develop a proposal for . . . ?
6. How would you deal with . . . ?
7. Invent a scheme that would . . .

Level VI: EVALUATION

1. In your opinion . . .
2. Appraise the chances for . . .
3. Grade or rank the . . .
4. What do you think should be the outcome?
5. What solution do you favor and why?
6. Which systems are best? Worst?
7. Rate the relative value of these ideas to . . .
8. Which is the better bargain?

POTENTIAL ACTIVITIES

1. Design a questionnaire about . . .
2. Conduct an investigation to produce . . .
3. Make a flowchart to show . . .
4. Construct a graph to show . . .
5. Put on a play about . . .
6. Review a work of art in terms of form, color, and texture.
7. Prepare a report about the area of study.

1. Create a model that shows your new ideas.
2. Devise an original plan or experiment for . . .
3. Finish the incomplete . . .
4. Make a hypothesis about . . .
5. Change . . . so that it will . . .
6. Propose a method to . . .
7. Prescribe a way to . . .
8. Give the book a new title.

1. Prepare a list of criteria you would use to judge a . . . Indicate priority ratings you would give.
2. Conduct a debate about an issue.
3. Make booklist about five rules you see as important. Convince others.
4. Form a panel to discuss . . .
5. Prepare a case to present your view about . . .
6. List some common statements about . . . that people often make. Are they accurate?

Figure 4.4   Verbs, Tasks, and Commands for the Six Sides of a Cube

Cubing . . . Levels of Thinking	
1. **Tell** **Describe** **Recall** **Name** **Locate** **List**	4. **Review** **Discuss** **Prepare** **Diagram** **Cartoon**
2. **Compare** **Contrast** **Example** **Explain** **Define** **Write**	5. **Propose** **Suggest** **Finish** **Prescribe** **Devise**
3. **Connect** **Make** **Design** **Produce** **Develop**	6. **Debate** **Formulate** **Choose** **Support** **In your opinion . . .**

How Do We Use Cubes?

- Keep clear learning goals in mind when considering the use of cubing for different learners.
- Provide extended opportunities, materials, and learning situations that provide a wide range of readiness, interests, and learning styles.
- Make sure students understand the verbs and directions for the tasks.
- Group students
  - o According to readiness with different-colored cubes, giving tasks or questions appropriate to their level of understanding and ability level in that particular topic or skill
  - o According to interest or choice
  - o Alone or with a partner, allowing students to assist one another in their learning

- Students may share findings with the large group or form base groups of experts to share their tasks.

Figure 4.5 Cubes Can Vary in Color and Tasks to Differentiate Learning

Green Cube	**Blue Cube**
1.	**1.**
2.	**2.**
3.	**3.**
4.	**4.**
5.	**5.**
6.	**6.**
Yellow Cube	**Red Cube**
1.	**1.**
2.	**2.**
3.	**3.**
4.	**4.**
5.	**5.**
6.	**6.**

SOURCE: Reprinted from *Differentiated Instructional Strategies: One Size Doesn't Fit All*, by Gayle H. Gregory and Carolyn Chapman. Thousand Oaks, CA: www.corwinpress.com

Differentiating With Cubes

Cubing may also be differentiated using multiple intelligences. Cubes may be designed with a variety of multiple intelligence activities to give students a chance to use their varied strengths. If students are studying the planets, for example, they might have a variety of cubes in the different multiple intelligences to process information such as cubes for musical/rhythmic intelligence, bodily/kinesthetic intelligence, visual/spatial intelligence, naturalist intelligence, logical/mathematical intelligence, or interpersonal or intrapersonal intelligences.

If colored cubes are being used to represent the visual/spatial multiple intelligence, students can be given the following statements on the six sides of their cubes:

Blue Cube

1. Draw . . .

2. Use a Venn diagram and compare . . .

3. Use a comic strip to tell what happened when . . .

4. Shut your eyes and describe_____. Draw what you see.

5. Predict what will_____. Use symbols.

6. In your opinion draw what will happen next.

Red Cube

1. Use a graphics program on the computer and create a character web for . . .

2. Use symbols on a Venn diagram to compare . . .

3. Use a storyboard to show . . .

4. Draw the _____and label the . . .

5. What is the message that you think the _____? Draw a symbol that illustrates your idea.

6. When you think of the title, do you agree or disagree that it is a good choice? Why or why not? Create a symbol to represent it.

Both the blue and red cubes are tapping into visual/spatial intelligence, with the blue cube working at a more basic level with key aspects. The red

Figure 4.6   Integrating Bloom's Taxonomy With Four Learning Styles

Thinking Level	Beach Ball	Microscope	Puppy	Clipboard
Knowledge	Draw or describe the scene.	Explain what . . .	Tell how you felt when . . .	In your own words tell . . . . List . . .
Comprehension	Create a poem or song to . . .	Write a report outlining . . .	Interview the characters.	Compare and contrast . . . using a Venn or other organizer.
Application	Write an original . . .	Use an essay or graphic to show . . .	Present your ideas about . . . to a small group.	Considering the reading, what are the basic . . .
Analysis and Synthesis	Finish the story with another ending.	Predict what will happen if . . .	Propose a solution that would deal with . . .	Outline what would come next.
Evaluation	Prepare a position for . . .	Debate the merits of . . .	Prescribe a compromise.	Rank the . . .

cube is stretching student thinking in the abstract, expanding ideas, and making connections.

Figure 4.6 suggests how teachers can set up assignments based on Bloom's taxonomy that also consider the diversity of learning styles and preferences. Students can choose one assignment at each thinking level and at least one from each style column. Many of these suggestions also tap into the various multiple intelligences.

Quellmalz's Thinking Taxonomy

E. S. Quellmalz (1985) offers a thinking taxonomy with five levels that is somewhat similar to Bloom's:

- Recall
- Analysis
- Comparison
- Inference
- Evaluation

Figure 4.7 illustrates the levels in Quellmalz's taxonomy, offering a definition of each level and trigger words for student thinking.

Figure 4.7   Trigger Words for Quellmalz's Thinking Taxonomy

Level	Definition	Trigger Words
Recall Repeating information	Recall is evidence of understanding and comprehension Expressing concepts, ideas, and principles in own words	Paraphrase Retell Repeat Restate Express in another way or form
Analysis Whole to parts	Dividing into component parts Characteristics or sequence may be included in analysis	Parts to whole Relationships Cause and effect Sequencing
Comparison Likes/differences	Emphasizing the similarities and differences between and among parts of ideas or objects	Similarities Differences Analogies Metaphors Synectics
Inference Generalizing	Combining the parts to draw conclusions or to make generalizations	Predicting Hypothesizing Concluding Synthesizing Deducing Inferring
Evaluation Judging	Judging the worth, quality, and credibility of an idea using a set of criteria and then supporting or justifying their conclusions	Assembling Explaining Rationalizing Providing evidence Justification

Tools and Organizers

Both Bloom's (1956) and Quellmalz's (1985) taxonomies allow us to help students think more deeply and diversely at a variety of levels. This active rehearsal and consideration of a topic from different points of view can also increase their understanding and retention of the information they are processing.

For example, the levels of thinking could be used while students are viewing a videotape. Figure 4.8 offers an organizer that may be used to outline in advance what information students are looking for, and Figure 4.9 offers a note-taking and summarizing sheet. These organizers could also be used to reflect on a textbook chapter or to summarize and take notes on a guest speaker, movie, field trip, article, or Web site.

This kind of activity appeals to auditory, visual, and kinesthetic learners as well as to the verbal/linguistic, logical/mathematical, visual/spatial, bodily/kinesthetic, naturalist, interpersonal, and intrapersonal learners. If we added a theme song or rap to the mix we could also tap into musical/rhythmic intelligence.

Figure 4.8   Teacher Tool for Student Thinking: Advance Organizer

---

Unit Planning

Topic:_____

Standards:_____

_____

_____

Concepts:_____

_____

_____

Big ideas or questions for the unit:_____

_____

_____

General suggestions for the six levels of Bloom's taxonomy

Knowledge

1. Write seven questions that you are interested in exploring about _____.
2. Keep a vocabulary list of definitions and related terms for the topic.
3. What are seven things you learned about_____?
4. What would you like to learn more about?
5. What was your best or biggest surprise about this topic?

Comprehension

1. Create a word web about the topic.
2. Describe in your own words why this new information is important to you.
3. Summarize for the newspaper article what you learned about_____.
4. How will you go about answering some of your own questions?
5. Show in a diagram or poster what you know.

Application

1. Compare and contrast _____ with _____.
2. Interview _____ about _____. Write the questions for the interview to make sure you cover all the information needed.
3. Keep a timeline of the events in this unit, day by day.
4. Create a diorama or model to explain . . .
5. Role-play or demonstrate _____.

Analysis

1. Draw a mind map to show how the details of _____connect.
2. Create a tree diagram to show the information flow of _____.
3. What conclusions might you draw from this information?
4. Conduct an Internet search to find out what experts say about_____.
5. What are the major headings and subheadings of this topic?

Synthesis

1. Write a newscast copy to explain this topic to those you don't know about it.
2. Prepare a PowerPoint presentation with the key information.
3. Make an audiotape outlining the key points to remember.
4. Create a cartoon series to show_____.
5. Write a song or jingle of what you have learned about_____.

(Continued)

Figure 4.8 (Continued)

Evaluation

1. Select some important information that you learned and rationalize its value to society/you/the discipline.

2. Rank the seven most important learnings from this unit. Give a rationale for your ranking.

3. What was the most effective strategy that helped you learn this new material, and why did it work for you?

4. Argue the need for everyone to know this information. What predictions can you make about the value of this knowledge?

5. What was the most valuable resource for your learning? Person? Text? Internet? What attributes made it valuable?

Figure 4.9   Teacher Tool for Student Thinking: Note-Taking and Summarizing Sheet

Level of Thinking	Questions	Notes
Recall	List five facts you learned.	
Comprehension	Summarize the main ideas.	
Application	With a partner, discuss an interesting idea from the tape.	
Analysis	What is one thing you would question or don't agree with?	
Synthesis	Create a word web with the ideas in the video.	
Evaluation	What criteria would you use to judge this video? Use the criteria to grade the video out of 10.	

Choice Boards

Teachers can better ensure that students are thinking at a variety of levels by creating choice boards. Choice boards allow students to pick three learning activities in a row, or four corners, or to create a question of their own to answer (see Figure 4.10).

Figure 4.10   Choice Board for Student Thinking

Knowledge	Comprehension	Application
Who, what, where, when, why, which, recall, locate, repeat, label, name, recite, find, relate, identify, select, find, show	Define, outline, reword, reconstruct, understand, calculate, conceive, paraphrase, transpose, convert, explain, interpret, demonstrate, draw, illustrate, summarize, translate	Adapt, transfer, solve, relate, transform, apply, employ, manipulate, use, utilize, transplant, convert, organize, model, discover, translate, produce, make, diagram, debate
Synthesis Build, regroup, blend, mix, compound, make, generate, join, combine, originate, develop, structure, imagine, predict, propose, improve, adapt, minimize, maximize, develop	**Create your own question and answer it**	**Analysis** Examine, dissect, inspect, sort, classify, separate, analyze, take apart, break down, scrutinize, discover, function, distinguish
Comprehension Define, outline, reword, reconstruct, understand, calculate, conceive, paraphrase, transpose, convert, explain, interpret, demonstrate, draw, illustrate, summarize, translate	**Knowledge** Who, what, where, when, why, which, recall, locate, repeat, label, name, recite, find, relate, identify, select, find, show	**Synthesis** Build, regroup, blend, mix, compound, make, generate, join, combine, originate, develop, structure, imagine, predict, propose, improve, adapt, minimize, maximize, develop

KRATHWOHL'S AFFECTIVE TAXONOMY

Another framework for thinking covers the affective domain. According to Beane (1985–86), *affect* refers to the conduct of humans that has to do with emotions, feelings, values, attitudes, predispositions, and morals. Naisbitt (1982) suggests that in this high-tech age, we need to be sure we include "heart-tech" to balance impersonal technology with humanness.

Educators often feel pressed to "cover the curriculum," which is "jam-packed" with outcomes and standards that focus on semantic information. It's not that we have to add a separate and extra curriculum for the affective skills, but rather, we can infuse or embed them in the existing programs. Benjamin S. Bloom and David R. Krathwohl developed a meaningful affective taxonomy (Krathwohl et al., 1964), although this was a difficult task because many educators believe that affective outcomes are very personal (Purdom, 1984).

Figure 4.11 Progression Through the Five Levels of Internalization

Level	Internalization
1. Receiving	Aware of a quality and will to pay attention to it
2. Responding	Reacts as expected with this quality
3. Valuing	Feels positive about the quality
4. Organization	Integrates quality with their personal system
5. Characterization	Part of their belief system

NOTE: To read more about this, see Krathwohl et al. (1964) and Purdom (1984).

Five Levels of the Affective Domain

According to Krathwohl's (Krathwohl et al., 1964) taxonomy, the five levels of the affective domain are the following:

1. **Receiving:** an awareness of feeling, attitude, or disposition of the learner

2. **Responding:** responding and garnering satisfaction from a feeling, attitude, or disposition of the learner

3. **Valuing:** making a commitment to a feeling, attitude, or disposition of the learner

4. **Organizing:** designing a set of values that are personal to a feeling, attitude, or disposition of the learner

5. **Characterizing:** being held accountable to a consistent set of personal values that have a feeling, attitude, or disposition of the learner

Purdom (1984) used the term *internalization* to show the progression from one level to another (see Figure 4.11), and the Internalization Chart in Figure 4.12 shows the five levels along with their operational definitions as well as key words to trigger the affective thinking.

Example

Let's look at an example of how the taxonomy works. Let's consider the quality of *responsibility.*

1. At the **receiving level,** the student is aware of the quality by noticing, listening, and observing people or a situation displaying this quality or lack of it.

Figure 4.12   Internalization Chart With Affective Trigger Words

Affective Goal	Operational Definition	Affective Trigger Words	
1. **Receiving:** pays attention	Listens, notices, observes	Be alert Be aware Be conscious Experience Handle Hear Heed	Listen Look Notice Observe Scan Perceive Watch
2. **Responding:** willingness to respond	Discussion, explanation	Answer Argue Attempt Comply Contribute Participate Cooperate Discuss Volunteer	Find Follow Gather Offer Express Proceed Submit Suggest Try
3. **Valuing:** accepting and preferring	Choosing	Adopt Advocate Approve Assign worth Choose Decide Defend	Honor Pick Promote Rank Propose Rate Embrace
4. **Organization:** recognizes and organizes	Reviews, questions, and arranges	Advocate Appraise Arrange Assess Coordinate Classify Compare Design Determine Establish order	Figure out Organize Propose Review Scheme Sort out Structure Systemize Plan Group
5. **Characterization:** internalization	Voices and affirms	Accept Adopt Avoid Confide in Trust Transact Testify Revise Re-act Reject	Act out Affirm Behave Declare Develop Disclose Do Proceed Resist Regulate

2. At the **responding level,** the student would want to discuss his or her views about responsibility.

3. At the **valuing level,** the student would choose to be responsible if given the choice.

4. At the **organizing level,** the student would, through reflection and review, integrate the quality into his or her value system.

5. At the **characterization level,** the student would advocate for the quality of responsibility and affirm its value.

Teachers can brainstorm other qualities to select and integrate into the curriculum for a term or a semester—for example, responsibility, persistence, reliability, and others. The students can be guided and coached through the stages of internalization in any subject discipline. Using metacognitive strategies is key to monitoring the internalization of the affective qualities of the Krathwohl taxonomy.

TEACHER ANALYSIS OF THINKING LEVELS

If you teach in a self-contained classroom at a grade level and teach all subjects to your students, Figure 4.13 (Bloom's taxonomy) and Figure 4.14 (Quellmalz's taxonomy) offer tools that may be applicable for assessing your use of the thinking levels. If you are a subject teacher and teach only one discipline, you will not need all the subject categories listed in the first column of each chart.

Conducting Your Analysis

1. For each subject, jot down all the activities you had students engage in for the week or in a particular unit of study in Column 2 labeled *Activities.* You may need to list more than six activities.

2. In the Verbs column, jot down the verb related to the activity.

3. In the fourth column, labeled Bloom's Level, select the number that corresponds to the verbs at any of the Bloom's six levels in Column 5.

4. After you have filled in the corresponding number from Bloom's 6, peruse the fourth column to see—
   - What level you have spent the most time in?
   - Which levels have you spent little time in?
   - Which levels have you spent no time in?

5. As a result of this information, what can you do about adding more levels or varying the levels in the unit for next time?

6. What will you do in the next unit to ensure better thinking at a variety of levels?

Figure 4.13   Teacher Analysis of Bloom's Thinking Levels

Subject	Activities	Verbs	Bloom's Level	Bloom's 6
Language Arts	1. 2. 3. 4. 5. 6.	1. 2. 3. 4. 5. 6.		**1. Knowledge** Who, what, where, why, when, which, recall, locate, repeat, label, name, recite, find, relate, identify, show, select
Science	1. 2. 3. 4. 5. 6.	1. 2. 3. 4. 5. 6.		**2. Comprehension** Define, outline, reword, reconstruct, understand, calculate, conceive, paraphrase, transpose, convert, explain, interpret, demonstrate, draw, illustrate, summarize, translate
Reading	1. 2. 3. 4. 5. 6.	1. 2. 3. 4. 5. 6.		**3. Application** Adapt, transfer, solve, relate, transform, apply, employ, make, manipulate, use, utilize, transplant, convert, organize, model
Math	1. 2. 3. 4. 5. 6.	1. 2. 3. 4. 5. 6.		**4. Analysis** Examine, dissect, inspect, sort, classify, separate, analyze, take apart, break down, scrutinize, discover, function, distinguish
Social Studies	1. 2. 3. 4. 5. 6.	1. 2. 3. 4. 5. 6.		**5. Synthesis** Build, regroup, blend, mix, compound, make, generate, join, combine, originate, develop, structure, imagine, predict, propose, improve, adapt, minimize, maximize, develop
Art	1. 2. 3. 4. 5. 6.	1. 2. 3. 4. 5. 6.		**6. Evaluation** Judge, weigh, decide, rate, rank, grade, arbitrate, determine, assess, appraise, disprove, justify, support, estimate, interpret

Figure 4.14 Teacher Analysis of Quellmalz's Thinking Levels

Subject	Activities	Verbs	Quellmalz's Level	Quellmalz's 5
Language Arts	1. 2. 3. 4. 5. 6.	1. 2. 3. 4. 5. 6.		**1. Recall** Paraphrase Retell Repeat Restate Express in another way or form
Science	1. 2. 3. 4. 5. 6.	1. 2. 3. 4. 5. 6.		**2. Analysis** Parts to whole Relationships Cause and effect Sequencing
Reading	1. 2. 3. 4. 5. 6.	1. 2. 3. 4. 5. 6.		**3. Comparison** Similarities Differences Analogies Metaphors Synectics
Math	1. 2. 3. 4. 5. 6.	1. 2. 3. 4. 5. 6.		**4. Inference** Predicting Hypothesizing Concluding Synthesizing Deducing Inferring
Social Studies	1. 2. 3. 4. 5. 6.	1. 2. 3. 4. 5. 6.		**5. Evaluation** Assembling Explaining Rationalizing Providing evidence Justification
Art	1. 2. 3. 4. 5. 6.	1. 2. 3. 4. 5. 6.		

Dimensions of Critical Thought

Paul and Elder (2001) identify 15 dimensions of critical thought:

Affective skills or skills related to the following:

1. Independent thinking
2. Developing insight into egocentricity or sociocentricity
3. Exercising fair-mindedness
4. Exploring thoughts underlying feelings and feelings underlying thoughts
5. Developing intellectual humility and suspending judgment

Cognitive—macro abilities

6. Clarifying issues, conclusions, or beliefs
7. Clarifying and analyzing the meanings of words or phrases
8. Developing criteria for evaluation: clarifying values and standards
9. Evaluating the credibility of sources of information
10. Analyzing or evaluating arguments, interpretations, beliefs, or theories
11. Listening critically: the art of silent dialogue

Cognitive—micro skills

12. Noting significant similarities and differences
13. Distinguishing relevant from irrelevant facts
14. Making plausible inferences, predictions, or interpretations
15. Evaluating evidence and alleged facts

Learning Pyramid

The learning pyramid has been around a long time. If we use a learning pyramid to organize research from the National Training Labs (NTL) in Bethel, Maine, about retention rates, we can see that teaching techniques such as discussion, practice, and teaching others lead to higher retention rates (see Figure 4.15).

If we use the different rates from the NTL research and then add different types of thinking such as Bloom's taxonomy, we can then use those findings to match our teaching strategies to the student learning styles (see Figure 4.16).

Figure 4.15   Average Retention Rates for Instructional Strategies

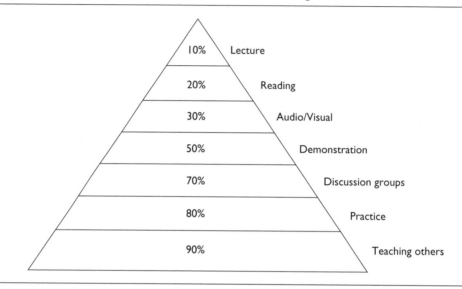

Figure 4.16   Instructional Strategies, Thinking Levels, and Learning Styles

People Retain	Bloom's	Strategies	Styles
10% Lecture	Knowledge	Lecturette Presentation Talk Guest speaker	Auditory Clipboard Microscope
20% Reading	Knowledge Comprehension	Text Internet Books Source materials	Visual Clipboard Microscope
30% Audiovisual	Knowledge Comprehension	Overhead Charts Diagrams PowerPoint Pictures Video/DVD Movie Audiotape/CD	Auditory/visual
50% Demonstration	Knowledge Comprehension Application	Teacher demonstration	Auditory/visual
70% Discussion	Knowledge Comprehension Analysis Synthesis	Partner sharing Small-group learning	Auditory Intrapersonal Verbal/linguistic Puppy

People Retain	Bloom's	Strategies	Styles
80% Practice	Knowledge Comprehension Application Analysis Synthesis	Practicing skills Verbal rehearsal Hands on Manipulatives Models Projects and centers	Auditory/visual Bodily/kinesthetic Beach ball Clipboard
90% Teaching others	Knowledge Comprehension Application Analysis Synthesis Evaluation	Student: Demonstrations Presentations Exhibitions Small-group learning	Auditory Interpersonal Verbal/linguistic Puppy Clipboard Microscope Beach ball

GRAPHIC ORGANIZERS TO SHOW THINKING

Marzano, Pickering, and Pollock (2001) found that graphic organizers (included in nonlinguistic representations) increase student achievement with the possibility of 37 percentile gains.

Students need to be introduced to the use of a particular organizer with simple content. Then they might be able to use it with more complex or unknown material. Eventually, students will be able to select the most appropriate organizer for the situation. The graphic organizers that follow are aligned with particular thinking skills.

Prioritizing or Ranking Ladder

A priority ladder is a useful tool to rank items. The highest-rated item is placed at the top of the ladder with those in descending importance placed on each rung below, with the least important one at the bottom of the ladder. Students may rank the topics of interest around a particular topic. They may rank their preferences in writing genre. They may rank the causes of the Vietnam War in order of importance and then give evidence or reasons for their ranking. It could also be used as an organizer for ranking the order of ideas for a writing assignment or prioritizing the order of steps for planning a project.

Sequencing Organizer

Sequencing is similar to a flowchart, timeline, or storyboard (see Figure 4.17). It can be used to show a chain of events or relationships between the steps in a process. This could be used as an organizer in a prewriting planning session. This can also be done using sticky notes so that they can be moved around and reordered easily if necessary.

Figure 4.17   Sequencing Organizer

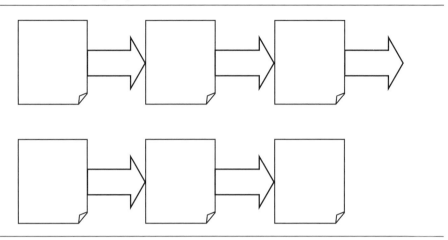

Word Web

This graphic could be used to show attributes or to brainstorm. Students could use it to build synonyms for a vocabulary word, attributes for a type of rock in earth sciences, or a character or historical figure. A more complex version can have subtopics that have minor themes off the original central concept or idea. It can show relationships and associations (see Figure 4.18).

Figure 4.18   Word Web

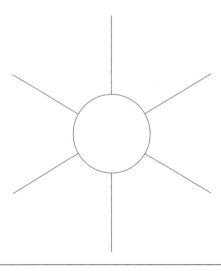

Figure 4.19   Pinwheel

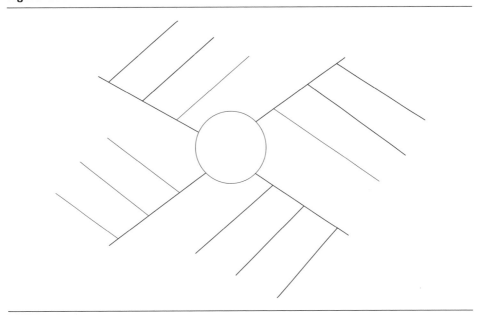

Pinwheel

The pinwheel is used for classifying and organizing information related to a topic or concept. The concept is placed in the center and a derivative or attribute is placed on each arm of the pinwheel. Then characteristics of each arm are added to the radial spokes (see Figure 4.19).

For example, the center bubble might have the name of a country the students are studying such as Greece and then each arm could be labeled: People, Historical Events, Geography, Famous People.

Compare and Contrast

Similarities and differences, comparing and contrasting are identified in the Marzano, Pickering, et al. (2001) research as having the capability of raising student achievement 43 percentile gains.

Organizers for this thinking skill can take many forms. The brain stores by similarities and retrieves by differences, thus this thinking skill adds in understanding and remembering attributes.

Venn Diagram: Circles and Boxes

John Venn introduced the circular diagram years ago for use in mathematics. The two intersecting circles each represent a set (see Figure 4.20).

Figure 4.20   Venn Diagram

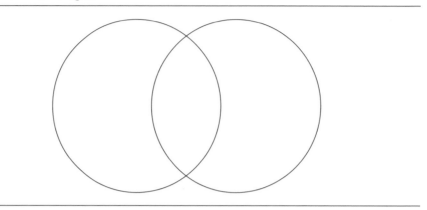

Figure 4.21   Boxing

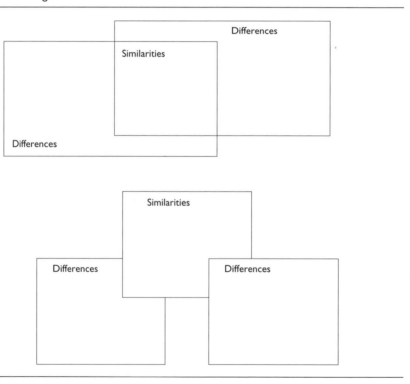

Characteristics unique to each set are kept in the outside part of each circle with the center holding the shared attributes. When three sets are compared, then three circles are used. Boxing is the same as the Venn except in rectangular form (see Figure 4.21).

Flowchart

The flowchart can also be used to compare and contrast. Each side deals with one topic. The elements being compared are placed in the arrows. The similarities for each element are placed in the oval in the center column with the differences in the rectangles on each side. If we were comparing Greece and Egypt, for example (see Figure 4.22), we might consider food, religion, government, and the like as elements to place within each of the arrows.

This flowchart would work for any two topics, ideas, or concepts to be compared—for example, the plot, setting, and theme of two stories or novels, with the attributes to be considered for comparison placed in the arrows. A template for other comparisons is provided as Figure 4.23.

Figure 4.22   Compare and Contrast Flowchart: Greece and Egypt

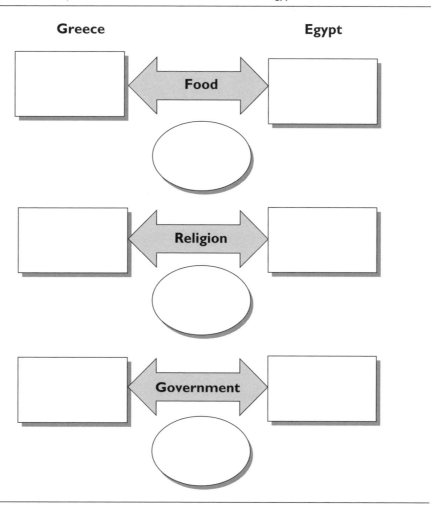

Figure 4.23   Compare and Contrast Flowchart: Template

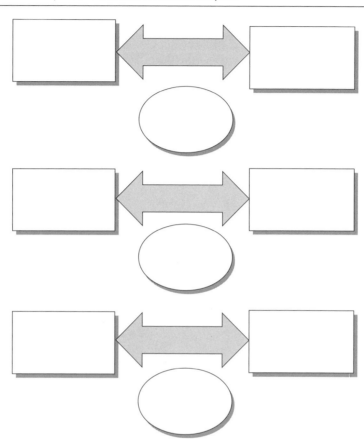

Fishbone

This organizer is often used to show cause and effect or to organize elements and characteristics related to a theme or topic. The problem or desired effect is placed in the "head" of the fish. Then the information or suggested solutions are placed in each section of the fishbone. It can be used as a note-taking and summarizing graphic as well, as seen in Figure 4.24. An American president's name can be placed in the fish head, and then each element can be examined and listed on the bones of the fish.

Right-Angle Reflection

As in the name, the right angle sets thinking at a tangent. The facts about topic are placed to the right of the horizontal arrow, and the reactions to or

Figure 4.24   Fishbone Organizer: American President

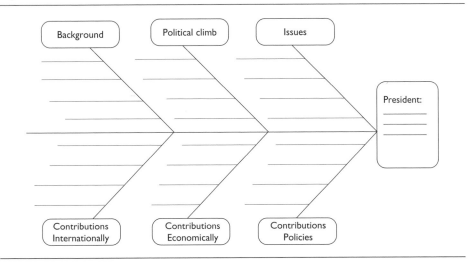

Figure 4.25   Right-Angle Reflection

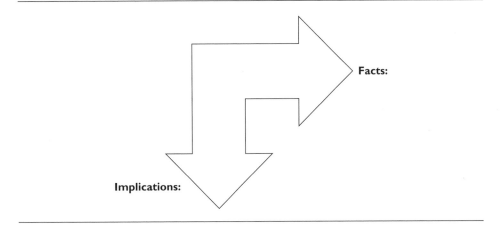

implications of the facts at the bottom of the vertical arrow (see Figure 4.25). For example, students could jot down the facts or events in a chapter of a novel and then predictions that they infer from the incident. It could be their personal reactions or feelings related to an event.

De Bono's Thinking Lenses

Edward de Bono's six lenses for examination method (de Bono, 1999) can be used to create assignments that ask students to view a video or read

Figure 4.26 Six Lenses for Creative Critical Thinking

White Lens	**Purple Lens**
• Hard facts • Figures • Data • Cold, neutral • Information	• Negative/down side • Why it won't work • Flaws and faults • What's wrong • Cautions
Red Lens	**Yellow Lens**
• Hunches • Intuition • Emotions • Feelings	• Positive aspects • Optimism • Enthusiasm • Constructive ideas • Benefits
Green Lens	**Blue Lens**
• Creative • Options • Choices • Beyond the obvious	• Conclusions • Summarizing statements • Definition • Sets

NOTE: For more information about Edward de Bono's Six Hat Thinking theory, see de Bono (1987, 1999).

an article through a particular lens (see Figure 4.26). Conversely, a different color of lens may be given to groups of students so the members of the group are all viewing and processing using the same slant or perspective. The teacher can use the lenses to increase student thinking beyond the factual, thus appealing to different learning styles and increasing thinking to a variety of levels.

Figure 4.27 offers a chart with room for questions that students can ponder related to a topic on the course of study. Students can also prepare questions for themselves or others to investigate as shown in the sample lesson on slavery (Figure 4.28).

Jigsaw Strategy

The six lenses can be used for jigsaw group work around a particular focus—for example, a textbook chapter, a video, an event, or situation (Figure 4.29). Each student can use a different color lens to collect information. Students would then bring that information to a discussion to share ideas and dialogue, and then they could make notes, create a graphic organizer, prepare a news release or TV bulletin, or create a poster. That way, there are options for the satisfaction of each group and attention to

Figure 4.27 Questions for Six Thinking Lenses

Thinking Lenses		
White Lens Pure white facts	Just the facts! Information Details Truths Computer like	
Purple Lens Judgment	The down side! What's wrong? Why it won't work Errors or mistakes	
Red Lens Just feel it	How do you feel? Emotions Get it out there Hunches Opinion	
Green Lens Green and growing	Where can this go? Growth Creative New "seeds"	
Yellow Lens Sunshine, brightness	Look on the bright side! Positive Up side Constructive Possibilities	
Blue Lens Cool and control	Pulling things together? Thinking about thinking Director of thinking Summaries	

visual, auditory, and kinesthetic learners. It also gives a chance to build in the eight multiple intelligences.

Choice Boards

Choice boards can also be created using thinking lenses to examine a topic from a variety of perspectives. Figure 4.30 offers a template that may

Figure 4.28   Sample Lesson for Six Thinking Lenses: Slavery

White Lens		What conditions led to slavery? Cite examples of reparations given to other groups. Describe the specific travel routes out of the south?
Purple Lens		What were three reasons why reparations will not work? What were the consequences for the people harboring the slaves?
Green Lens		Besides money, what other reparations can be made to descendents of African Americans? How were families affected after finding freedom in the north?
Red Lens		How do you feel about reparations? Interview three adults about how they feel about reparations.
Yellow Lens		What are the benefits of reparations?
Blue Lens		Make a timeline of events/laws showing discrimination that would justify reparations. What would the United States presently be if the Underground Railroad never existed?

Figure 4.29   Jigsaw Organizer for Six Thinking Lenses

White Lens Just the facts! • Hard facts • Figures • Data • Cold, neutral • Information	
Purple Lens Negative/down side • Why it won't work • Flaws and faults • What's wrong • Cautions	
Green Lens Creative • Options • Choices • Beyond the obvious	
Red Lens Just feel it • Hunches • Intuition • Emotions • Feelings	

Yellow Lens
Positive aspects
  • Optimism
  • Enthusiasm
  • Constructive ideas
  • Benefits	

Blue Lens
Conclusions
  • Summarizing statements
  • Definition
  • Sets	

Figure 4.30   Choice Board Template for Thinking Lenses

1. **White** Factual Information	2. **Purple** Judgment Downside	3. **Green** Possibilities Growth
4. **Blue** Reflective and summarizing	**Wild Card!**	5. **Red** Feelings and emotions
6. **Yellow** Values and benefits	7. **White** Factual Information	8. **Blue** Reflective and summarizing

be used to create a choice board, Figure 4.31 offers a sample choice board for a unit on *Little House on the Prairie,* and Figure 4.32 shows a sample unit on the Civil Rights Movement.

Notice that the six thinking lenses have been used but that there is also evidence of multiple intelligence preferences and a variety of thinking skills as well as a conscious effort to include auditory, visual, and kinesthetic activities.

Figure 4.31   Sample Choice Board for *Little House on the Prairie*

When was Laura Ingalls Wilder born? White Lens	**Describe** three challenges the family faced. Purple Lens	**Describe** one challenge in **detail**. How would the story be **different** if they did not face this challenge? Green Lens
What would Laura need to adjust to if she lived today? Yellow Lens	**Wild Card!**	Describe how Laura **felt** when Mary went blind. Red Lens
What **positive message** can you take from these books? Blue Lens	**Describe** the town of Walnut Grove (use pictures or words). White Lens	What challenges did Mary face when she went blind? How would meeting those challenges be different today? Purple Lens

Figure 4.32   Sample Choice Board for the Civil Rights Movement

Who were the leaders of the Civil Rights Movement?	What were the **negative viewpoints** of the people involved in the Civil Rights Movement? What were the regrets?	How could you **show** the Civil Rights Movement of yesterday, today, and tomorrow?
What were the **results** of the Civil Rights Movement?	**Wild Card!** **Free Choice**	How did you **feel** when you heard the "I have a dream" speech?
In what ways is America **better off** as a result of the Civil Rights Movement?	**What** was the Civil Rights Movement?	**Compare** the civil rights issues of today with the movement in its inception.

Plus, Minus, Interesting

One of de Bono's CoRT (1987) program processes is "plus, minus, interesting." It is a useful tool in analyzing what we think about or how we react to a situation, idea, or theory. Often we say to students, what do you think about that? And they don't know what to respond.

Giving students a framework and prompts (see Figure 4.33) to help their thinking makes them better thinkers. This kind of organizer allows students to pair up with a partner and respond to a theory, or they can react to a video, story, situation in history, finding in science, technique in art, a composition in music, a solution to a problem, or a play in a basketball game. A template is provided if you want to give prompts of your own (see Figure 4.34). Some teachers change *interesting* to *intriguing*.

Figure 4.33   Plus, Minus, Interesting Prompts

Plus	Minus	Interesting
What did you like about it? What's important here? What is the "up side" of this? This explains . . . This information is helpful because . . . Now I can . . .	The problem is . . . The "down side" of this is . . . What worries me . . . I'm still confused about . . . I'm concerned about . . .	I thought it was neat that . . . I never realized . . . I was surprised . . . It never occurred to me . . . Never before . . . Most unusual was . . . I'm intrigued by . . . That was a different . . . I'd never thought about . . .

Figure 4.34   Plus, Minus, Interesting Template

Plus	Minus	Interesting

CREATIVE THINKING

Some people are right at home thinking creatively. A safe environment where risk taking is encouraged is perfect for creative thinking to thrive. It allows one to be in a state of relaxed alertness and somewhat "off center." Also a great resource for creative thinking is the right hemisphere of the brain (see Chapter 1). The right hemisphere is always looking for unique and innovative ideas and ways to do things, but we are also using the left hemisphere to note details and to logically assess our creative ideas.

Creative thinking can be taught. And one of the most common ways to get the creative juices flowing is brainstorming.

Brainstorming

Because the brain stores information in networks of association, brainstorming is a way to let the connections flow and ideas be generated creatively. Brainstorming should be free flowing without discussion or judgments.

Flow

We can use FLOW to help the brainstorming process:

F Free flow of ideas

L Let all ideas come out, even off-the-wall ones

O Originality counts

W Weigh options later

Other suggestions for brainstorming include these:

1. Allow students to generate a few ideas individually so that they have something to share.

2. Limit the time for brainstorming to discourage evaluating ideas.

3. Encourage lots of ideas, original or piggybacking on the ideas of others.

Carousel Brainstorming (Kagan, 1992)

Paper is posted around the room with a topic or question or problem on each one. Students move from chart to chart at the signal and they brainstorm suggestions or solutions at each chart. One person records for each group using one color marker. Each group uses the same color marker on each chart so that when the brainstorming is over and the ideas are debated, the color will identify which group wrote the ideas.

Graffiti Brainstorming (Gibbs, 1995)

When graffiti brainstorming, the sheets of paper are placed on the table where each group is working, not on the wall. The sheets of paper are passed around from table to table rather than to have the groups moving. The rotations are timed so that the brainstorming is rapid and free flowing.

Williams's Creative Taxonomy

Frank Williams (1970, 1972, 1989, 1993) developed a taxonomy for creative thinking processes that has eight levels:

- Fluency
- Flexibility
- Originality
- Elaboration
- Risk taking
- Curiosity
- Imagination
- Complexity management

Figure 4.35 explains the learner expectations associated with the eight levels and suggests trigger words that can be used to prompt thinking in this venue. Teachers may use Williams's creativity taxonomy as they might use Bloom's or Quellmalz's taxonomies as a "touchstone" in planning to make sure they are consciously planning for all levels of thinking throughout a lesson or unit of study.

Although many tests are often at the recall level, standardized testing more and more requires that students think at various levels of the taxonomy and not only know the information but also apply, analyze, synthesize, and evaluate it. The creativity boards shown in Figures 4.36 and 4.37 use all

Figure 4.35 Trigger Words for Williams's Creative Taxonomy

Learner Expectations	Trigger Words	
Fluency is the ability to generate lots of ideas, answers, options, opinions, and choices in a given context.	Oodles Bunches Quantity Few	Scads Many Lots Multiple
Flexibility is the skill of adjusting, modifying, tapering, by varying size, shape, limits, quantities, objectives, dimensions, and perspectives.	Adapt Different Detour Redirect	Adjust Alternatives Variety Change
Originality is the skill of seeking the possibilities, through clever thinking and making novel changes that create the unusual or unobvious.	Unique Unusual New Unobvious	Clever Novel Innovative Unheard of
Elaborating is the skill that facilitates stretching through expansion, enlargement, enrichment, or embellishment by building on previous thinking.	Expand Embellish Build Add on	Embroider Stretch Enlarge Enrich
Risk taking is a skill that deals with experimentation, taking chances, or venturing forth into the unknown.	Try Explore Guess Estimate	Dare Predict Experiment Adventure

Figure 4.35 (Continued)

Learner Expectations	Trigger Words	
Complexity management is a skill that creates order out of chaos, structure in an illogical situation.	Solve Seek alternative Order	Improve Intricate Rank
Curiosity is a skill that allows one to question alternatives, follow up a hunch, intuit, or wonder about options.	Question Intuit Ask Follow a hunch	Wonder Inquire Ponder Suppose
Imagining is a skill used to visualize and build a picture in the mind, imagine possibilities and stretch beyond what is practical to produce what might be.	Fantasize Imagine Visualize Daydream	Wonder Dream Reach out

Figure 4.36   Creativity Board With Prompts for Williams's Taxonomy

Fluency	Flexibility	Originality
Name all . . . List as many . . . Think of as many uses . . . How many uses . . . List as many objects . . . Form as . . . Invent as many . . .	If . . . Classify . . . Group objects . . . What if . . . If someone . . . Describe as many . . . Think as many . . .	Think of a novel . . . Make up . . . Think of some practical . . . What clever ideas . . . Create four uses for . . . What are some ways . . .
Elaboration Build on this . . . Finish this . . . Add . . . Explain ways to . . . Elaborate on . . . If you could . . . Stretch your thinking by . . . Expand on this . . .	**Free Space**	**Risk Taking** Give three reasons for . . . Describe something . . . Pantomime . . . If you could dream . . . Pretend that . . . Rename . . . If you had two wishes . . . A time when . . .

Curiosity
What do you think . . .
What intrigues you about . . .
Who would you
  interview . . .
Pretend you are . . .
Invent a . . .
	Imagination
	Imagine that . . .
	Imagine if . . .
	Pretend that . . .
	If you had . . . did . . . could . . .
	Stretch your . . .
		Complexity
		What if . . .
		Describe how . . .
		If people had . . . If you
		  had . . .
		Explain all . . .
		When . . . what . . .
		Think of ways to . . .

Figure 4.37   Creativity Board Template for Williams's Taxonomy

Fluency	Flexibility	Originality
Elaboration	**Free Space**	Risk Taking
Curiosity	Imagination	Complexity

levels of Williams's taxonomy to encourage student thinking. Once the learning standards targeted for a unit of study have been considered, the template in Figure 4.37 may be used to design a unit or lesson around any topic.

Creative Reports

Novelty satisfies the brain, especially the brain of the beach ball learner and other learners who like variety and choice. The following types of reports can be novel ways of culminating, sharing, and celebrating the learning:

- ABC report
- The Reader's Digest approach
- Staggered-page flip book

- Comic book report
- A "Bloomin'" accordion
- Shoebox kit
- Shape book

These kinds of creative reports also incorporate auditory, visual, and kinesthetic preferences and attend to those multiple intelligences such as verbal/linguistic, visual/spatial, naturalist, logical/mathematical, interpersonal, and intrapersonal. Musical/rhythmic can also be included, because some students like to write in rhyme.

A creative report can also be a great metacognitive tool when we ask students to tell why they chose the information they included. Quantity can be adjusted to keep all students in the groove without overwhelming them or underrating their potential. These reports may be shared or displayed for all to see, hear, and examine. They also allow students to use their creative skills as well as their technological prowess in desktop publishing, PowerPoint, hypercard, and so on. Active processing and elaborate rehearsal of information are all part of these endeavors, thus aiding in long-term memory filing.

ABC Report

Using a different page for each letter of the alphabet, students can in visual and verbal form consolidate their thinking and the knowledge they have gained about the topic they have studied alphabetically. This can be done individually or in cooperative groups depending on the preference of the learner or the teacher. The interpersonal, puppy learner will probably jump at the chance to work with a peer or a small group. This assignment has a brainstorming aspect as well and gives students a chance to personalize the learning depending on what interested them the most or had the most impact.

Sample ABC reports might cover:

- ABC's of fractions
- ABC's of Colorado
- ABC's of fossils
- ABC's of the Civil War
- ABC's of personal fitness
- ABC's of substance abuse
- ABC's of grammar
- ABC's of America's mountain ranges

The Reader's Digest Approach

This can be set up in a magazine format, and students can work in a small group yet individually write on a topic of their choice, exhibiting

Figure 4.38   Staggered-Page Flip Book

what they have learned and what they may want to take further in their investigation. It allows those interpersonal students to conduct interviews, the microscope learner to go deeper into the content, and the beach ball learner to find the area of interest while still focusing on the content and the outcomes. It also has enough structure with flexibility to satisfy the clipboard and his or her colleagues.

The magazine will focus on the topic being studied and the articles, reports, and interviews will incorporate materials to substantiate the outcomes. The students are practicing literacy skills across the curriculum and will format the magazine with a table of contents, brief annotation of the articles, illustrations, graphs and charts as needed, and proper references for their work.

Staggered-Page Flip Book

First you need to decide how many pages you will need in the flip book. Using white paper or foolscap, line up the pages, staggering each page one inch above the edge of the last one, after you have placed the number of sheets needed. Then fold the pile of papers in half and cut on the fold. That will give you two books. Staple on the cut edge of each (see Figure 4.38).

Each sheet will deal with a different aspect of the topic. It could be a book on mountain ranges with one range on each sheet or on presidents or almost any topic that students are studying.

Comic Book Report

An 8.5- × 11-inch piece of paper may be used for the comic strip. Place it in front of you so that it is in the portrait position. Fold the paper in half and then in half again. That will create four sections. Then fold the paper

Figure 4.39   Comic Book Report

in half again to make eight sections or two rows for the comic strip of four sections in each row. Choose a topic and tell a story or retell an event in cartoon form. This is especially appealing for the visual/spatial artistic student who will enjoy rehearsing information and demonstrating under-standing in this way (see Figure 4.39).

A "Bloomin'" Accordion

Student-created assignments using levels of thinking can be turned into a book on a particular topic. Fold construction paper like an accordion in four sections or more. The front page will be the cover sheet, and each subsequent page will have a paragraph about the topic or perhaps a famous person. At the bottom of the page, there will be a question for the reader to answer. The question will be at a different level of Bloom's taxonomy preferable from the analysis, synthesis, and evaluation levels. The reader will read the paragraph and answer the question. Students can demonstrate understanding by asking good questions (see Figure 4.40).

Shoebox Kit

Students can create a shoebox on a topic of interest and choice. This can be a culminating project to show what they know or to teach another student about the topic. The student will decorate the shoebox on the theme and give it a title. The finished kit should contain the following:

Figure 4.40 "Bloomin'" Accordion

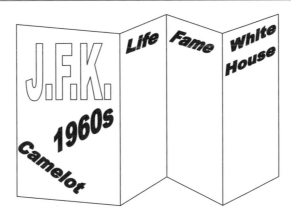

- A cover sheet
- A list of contents
- A few pages of information about the topic
- A word search or crossword puzzle to review the topic
- A glossary of terms
- A creative activity related to the topic
- A rubric to assess their learning
- A reflection sheet

Shape Book

A shape book takes the form of a familiar object such as an apple or a house or an animal and can be particularly appropriate for visual/spatial learners (see Figure 4.41).

Figure 4.41 Shape Book

SCAMPER

Bob Eberle (1982), a proponent of creative and critical thinking, developed SCAMPER as a method of thinking creatively about a topic or item.

SCAMPER is another brainstorming tool that uses a set of prompts to help the creativity flow. An expert in using thinking strategies, Eberle arranged his prompts in the following acrostic, which proves to be a useful mnemonic device:

S **ubstitute:** What procedures, methods, materials, personnel, places, or times can we use **in place of** this?

C **ombine:** What procedures, methods, materials, personnel, places, or times can we **add** to this?

A **dapt:** How can we **adapt** procedures, methods, materials, personnel, places, or times or put this to **another use**?

M **odify:** How can we **modify** procedures, methods, materials, personnel, places, or times to make this bigger, smaller, stronger, faster, flexible, lighter, and so on?

P **ut to other uses:** What can we do with this to use it in **other situations** for other **circumstances**?

E **liminate:** What can be **simplified** or **left out**?

R **everse:** Can this process or method or material be **turned around**? Could we start at the end or in another place?

SCAMPER can be used to solve problems through adaptation, combination, adjustment, modification, or elimination. Students can use this tool to "think outside the box" and let their creativity fly. They should be encouraged not to evaluate suggestions until all brainstorming has been completed. Evaluation during the brainstorming process limits thinking and inhibits the contributions of some who may not contribute if they feel their suggestions might be reacted to in a negative way.

It is often freeing to remind students that sometimes great ideas come from off-the-wall suggestions or even mistakes. SCAMPER can be a helpful tool for an environmental unit where students are discussing ways to recycle materials or reduce garbage or litter.

Daily Creativity

A creativity calendar can be an intriguing tool for teachers to keep creative thinking an ongoing classroom event. These may be "do now"

Figure 4.42 Prompts for a Month of Creative Thinking

Monday	Tuesday	Wednesday	Thursday	Friday
If I could choose how to spend today, I would ...	Draw how the earth changes in spring.	Pretend you are a mouse that people are trying to catch. Describe your life.	What would be the worst thing about living without water in your house?	Where is the moon in the daytime?
Imagine you could go to any country, which one would you choose and why?	Why is math like a language?	Think about something that confuses you. Try to make sense of it.	What intrigues you more—sand or sea?	List all the things you could do with a spoon.
Rename the appliances in your kitchen.	How do birds know where they are going?	Why do birds have different kinds of beaks and feet?	What interesting things could a rat tell you?	Does a tree make a noise when it falls in the forest?
Find a picture you like in a magazine and write a caption/story for it.	What would another method be to handle garbage rather than weekly collection?	Imagine you won a trip to Hong Kong. How would plan your time there?	If you didn't have buttons or a zipper on your coat how could you keep it fastened?	If you could plant a garden what would you put in it?
What would you put in a basic survival kit and why?	If there were an eighth day of the week, what would you call it and why do we need one?	Explain why salmon swim upstream.	Imagine you lived in a glass house. Would you like that? Why or why not?	Your best job would be a _____ because _____

prompts first thing in the morning to get students focused or, as some teachers say, provide "breakfast for the brain."

These creativity prompts can also be used for journal prompts to get students thinking in ways other than just recall or reaction. You can use the prompts provided in Figure 4.42, or you can create your own calendar for thinking that deals with topics your students are studying next month (see Figure 4.43). This can stimulate teacher thinking as well as student thinking. Better yet, have students contribute creative thinking ideas for next month's calendar.

Figure 4.43   Template to Create Your Own Month of Creative Thinking

Monday	Tuesday	Wednesday	Thursday	Friday

METACOGNITION: THINKING ABOUT OUR THINKING

Metacognition is thinking about our thinking. Metacognition behaviors may include the following:

- Posing questions of interest
- Comparing and contrasting information
- Monitoring personal progress

- Predicting what will come next and perhaps why
- Evaluating and judging

Swartz and Perkins (1990) suggest four levels of metacognitive behavior:

Level 1 Tacit use: Problem solves without reflective thinking on past experiences and strategies

Level 2 Aware use: Conscious use of a particular strategy

Level 3 Strategic use: Organized thinking with deliberation in selection and use of a particular strategy

Level 4 Reflective use: Plans, selects, monitors, and judges the use of a particular strategy

Metacognition and Reflection

Metacognition or reflection is more powerful than thinking itself. Metacognition encourages the thinker to make connections by conscious reflection. It also helps the thinker to master the thinking skills he or she is practicing. If the climate is safe, students will honestly judge their efforts and honestly set goals or make adjustments for the next attempt. In our haste to cover the curriculum, teachers need to make time for the important task of reflection.

The brain has information in an unconscious state in long-term memory and can be called up when needed:

- Sometimes it is at the **beginning** of a unit or lesson when we want to know what students **already know** or don't know about a topic or concept.
- Sometimes it is **during** the unit or lesson when we check for understanding.
- And sometimes it is **after** the learning when we want to bring closure.

Perkins (1995) suggests that reflective thinking has to be a focus if we expect students to practice metacognition and avoid gaps in their thinking. Damasio (1999) refers to metacognition as extended consciousness that increases with maturity as we expand our experiences.

Reflective strategies have to be taught. The following suggestions can be used to enhance reflective thinking:

- Model strategies to problem solve
- Encourage open-mindedness to others' ideas
- Foster objections as a way to examine new thoughts
- Remember personal experiences to help decision making
- Look for and identify patterns

Feedback

Exit Slips

When teachers solicit feedback at the end of class, they sometimes use a "ticket out" or an "exit slip." They may ask any number of questions or offer prompts to help students reflect on their learning:

- What was perfectly clear to you today?
- What is still a little out of focus?
- What are you wondering about?
- What was easy for you today?
- What was challenging? Difficult? Frustrating? Puzzling?
- What more would you like to know?
- How might it have been more interesting for you?
- What would have made the learning more fun, interesting, better?
- What do you still want to know?
- What are two things you learned today?
- What is one question you still have?

Logs and Journals

Using a T chart (see Figure 4.44), students can jot down some facts on the left side of the chart and their reactions or questions on the right side.

Figure 4.44   T Chart for Reflection

Facts	Opinions/Questions/Reactions

If students do not reflect on their work and behavior, they may continue to make the same errors in their work or their judgment. Some of the following prompts may help them reflect and set goals for the next time.

Assignment or Project Reflection

> I was asked to . . .
>
> The best thing about it was . . .
>
> I found . . . easy.
>
> I thought . . . difficult.
>
> I really learned that . . .
>
> I enjoyed . . .
>
> I don't enjoy . . .
>
> Next time I will . . .
>
> I need help with . . .

Making the Right Choices for Your Classroom

5

So what does this mean for teachers? Do we have to do all this in every lesson? How do we cope with the complexity of research and available models concerning learning preferences, learning styles, multiple intelligences, best practice, and thinking skills?

PLANNING FOR DIFFERENTIATED LEARNING

The reality is that we can use differentiated strategies to provide variety for our students, and we can use teacher reflection to examine our plans to see if we are attending to the diversity in our classrooms while also focusing on the standards.

Figure 5.1 provides a planning template that can be used to help teachers make decisions about differentiated instruction and thinking. Each phase of the planning will be explained, and then we will look at a sample lesson scenario to critique and reflect on teacher choices (see Figure 5.2).

Step 1: Standards

The first thing to be considered, of course, will be the standards or outcomes being targeted in the lesson. It is imperative that students share in the objective and purpose of the learning. They should know what the teacher expects them to know, be able to do, or be like.

Figure 5.1   Template for Planning Differentiated Learning

PLANNING FOR DIFFERENTIATED LEARNING		
Unit title:	**Grade level:**	
STANDARDS: What should students know and be able to do for this portion of the unit?	**Preassessment lesson strategy:** Use the data from the adjustable grid designed from unit preassessment tool to start the unit and data from formative assessments throughout the unit, such as journals, ticket out, quick writes, quizzes.	
CRITICAL QUESTION FOR THIS PORTION OF THE UNIT:	**Personal Question(s):**	
CONTENT: (Concepts)	**SKILLS: (What will students do?)**	
ACTIVATE: (Creating focus and purpose)		Quiz, Test, Survey, K.W.L. journals, Brainstorm concept, Formation, Four corner graphic
ACQUIRE: (Getting the information total or small groups) (learning styles, multiple intelligences)		Lecturette, Demonstration, Presentation, Jigsaw, Video, Field trip, Guest speaker, Text
APPLY ADJUST: TAPS, random, heterogeneous, homogeneous, interest, task, constructed	Bloom Quellmalz Williams Krathwohl	Learning centers, Projects, Contracts, Compact/enrich, Problem based, Inquiry, Research, Independent study
ASSESS:		Quiz, Test, Rubric, Performance, Products, Presentation, Journal, Demonstration, Log

Figure 5.2   Sample Lesson on Mammals for Second Grade

PLANNING FOR DIFFERENTIATED LEARNING

Unit title: Mammals	Grade level: Two
STANDARDS: What should students know and be able to do for this portion of the unit?	**Preassessment lesson strategy:** Use the data from the adjustable grid designed from unit preassessment tool to start the unit and data from formative assessments throughout the unit, such as journals, ticket out, quick writes, quizzes.
CRITICAL QUESTION FOR THIS PORTION OF THE UNIT: **What is a mammal?**	**Personal Question(s):**
CONTENT: (Concepts)	**SKILLS: (What will students do?)**
ACTIVATE: (Creating focus and purpose)	Quiz, Test, Survey, K.W.L. journals, Brainstorm concept, Formation, Four corner graphic
ACQUIRE: (Getting the information total or small groups) (learning styles, multiple intelligences)	Lecturette, Demonstration, Presentation, Jigsaw, Video, Field trip, Guest speaker, Text
APPLY ADJUST: TAPS, random, heterogeneous, homogeneous, interest, task constructed	Learning centers, Projects, Contracts, Compact/enrich, Problem based, Inquiry, Research, Independent study
ASSESS:	Quiz, Test, Rubric, Performance, Products, Presentation, Journal, Demonstration, Log

Step 2: Content

Content will be identified, including the facts and concepts as well as the essential skills.

Step 3: Activate

Teachers will design tools to access prior knowledge and to preassess so that planning will be more precise. This could be done enough time ahead of the lesson to allow for accurate planning: grouping of students, strategies that match the content and the students' learning styles and multiple intelligences. Novelty may be used to "hook" students' interest and curiosity about the topic.

Step 4: Acquire

Teachers will make decisions about what new information and skills are needed for which students. Teachers will decide what will be taught to the whole class, to individuals, to partners, or to small groups.

Step 5: Apply and Adjust

Application and practice will give students the chance to become actively engaged with the new learning and use the levels of thinking in the process. This may vary based on students' readiness or interests and on challenging them at the appropriate level.

Step 6: Assess

The teacher will decide (or provide choices) so that students can demonstrate their learning.

Putting It All Together

These decisions are made with the diversity of the students in mind: their learning styles, their thinking styles, their multiple intelligences, and more.

Figure 5.2 offers a sample lesson scenario. In a second-grade class-room, the teacher was focusing on a science unit about mammals. Because of the interests of the students, they were working in groups based on animals they were interested in studying. The teacher had used a survey a few days ahead of the unit to find out student preferences and interests for the unit.

REFLECTING ON DIFFERENTIATED INSTRUCTIONAL PLANNING

Is This Lesson/Unit Brain Compatible?

Use the BRAIN checklist (Figure 5.3) as a reflection tool to evaluate this sample unit.

Figure 5.3   Checklist of Brain-Compatible Questions for Teachers Planning Differentiated Learning for Their Students

B uilding safe environments

- o Do students feel safe to risk and experiment with ideas?
- o Do students feel included in the class and supported by others?
- o Are tasks challenging enough without undo or "dis" stress?
- o Is there an emotional "hook" for the learners?
- o Are there novel, unique, and engaging activities to capture and sustain attention?
- o Are "unique brains" honored and provided for? (learning styles & multiple intelligences)

R ecognizing and honoring diversity

- o Does the learning experience appeal to the learners' varied and multiple intelligences and learning styles?
- o May the students work collaboratively and independently?
- o May they "show what they know" in a variety of ways?
- o Does the cultural background of the learners influence instruction?

A ssessment

- o Are preassessments given to determine readiness?
- o Is there enough time to explore, understand, and transfer the learning to long-term memory (grow dendrites)? Is there time to accomplish mastery?
- o Do they have opportunities for ongoing, "just in time" feedback?
- o Do they have time to revisit ideas and concepts to connect or extend them?
- o Is metacognitive time built into the learning process?
- o Do students use logs and journals for reflection and goal setting?

I nstructional Strategies

- o Are the expectations clearly stated and understood by the learner?
- o Will the learning be relevant and useful to the learner?
- o Does the learning build on past experience or create a new experience?
- o Does the learning relate to their real world?
- o Are strategies developmentally appropriate and hands on?
- o Are the strategies varied to engage and sustain attention?
- o Are there opportunities for projects, creativity, problems, and challenges?

N umerous Curriculum Approaches

- o Do students work alone, in pairs, and in small groups?
- o Do students work in learning centers based on interest, need, or choice?
- o Are some activities adjusted to provide appropriate levels of challenge?
- o Is pre-testing used to allow for compacting/enrichment?
- o Are problems, inquiries, and contracts considered?

Does This Lesson/Unit Tap a Variety of Multiple Intelligences?

Use the palette of multiple intelligences suggestions (Figure 5.4) as a reflection tool to evaluate the sample unit.

Figure 5.4 A Palette of Suggestions for Using the Eight Multiple Intelligences

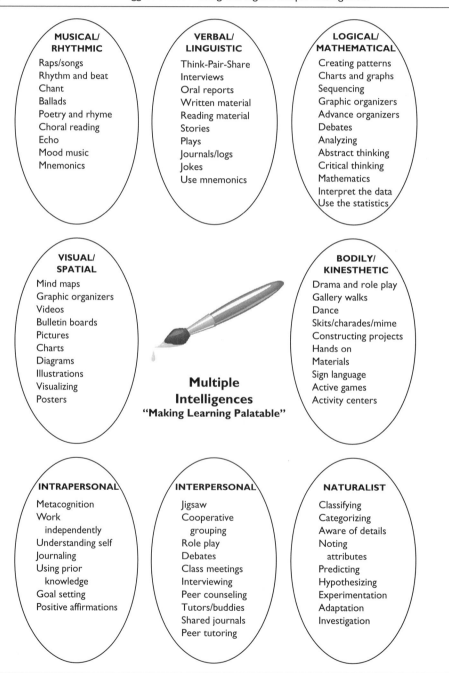

MUSICAL/ RHYTHMIC
Raps/songs
Rhythm and beat
Chant
Ballads
Poetry and rhyme
Choral reading
Echo
Mood music
Mnemonics

VERBAL/ LINGUISTIC
Think-Pair-Share
Interviews
Oral reports
Written material
Reading material
Stories
Plays
Journals/logs
Jokes
Use mnemonics

LOGICAL/ MATHEMATICAL
Creating patterns
Charts and graphs
Sequencing
Graphic organizers
Advance organizers
Debates
Analyzing
Abstract thinking
Critical thinking
Mathematics
Interpret the data
Use the statistics

VISUAL/ SPATIAL
Mind maps
Graphic organizers
Videos
Bulletin boards
Pictures
Charts
Diagrams
Illustrations
Visualizing
Posters

BODILY/ KINESTHETIC
Drama and role play
Gallery walks
Dance
Skits/charades/mime
Constructing projects
Hands on
Materials
Sign language
Active games
Activity centers

Multiple Intelligences
"Making Learning Palatable"

INTRAPERSONAL
Metacognition
Work
  independently
Understanding self
Journaling
Using prior
  knowledge
Goal setting
Positive affirmations

INTERPERSONAL
Jigsaw
Cooperative
  grouping
Role play
Debates
Class meetings
Interviewing
Peer counseling
Tutors/buddies
Shared journals
Peer tutoring

NATURALIST
Classifying
Categorizing
Aware of details
Noting
  attributes
Predicting
Hypothesizing
Experimentation
Adaptation
Investigation

Does This Lesson/Unit Offer
Something Satisfying for All Learning Styles?

Considering clipboards:

- There are clear directions and expectations.
- The environment is orderly, consistent, and efficient.
- The timeline of assignments and the grading guidelines are shared clearly and accurately.
- The materials are available, and models or samples are shown.
- Real experiences and genuine need is established.
- There are concrete examples, not just theories.
- The environment is structured, orderly, quiet.
- There are procedures, routines, and predictable situations.
- There are practical hands-on applications.
- There is guided practice for successful results.

Considering beach balls:

- They have a chance to make choices.
- They are able to be self-directed at some time.
- They are in a competitive situation on occasion.
- They are allowed to experiment through trial and error.
- They get a chance to brainstorm and deal with open-ended options.
- They have activities that are hands on.
- They are encouraged to create and use their imagination.

Considering puppies:

- There are opportunities to work with others.
- They have time for self-reflection.
- They get feedback and connect with the teacher and other learners.
- They have a rationale for the learning.
- They feel included and get some personal attention and support.
- The environment is safe to take risks and mostly is noncompetitive.
- Open communication exists and their ideas are accepted.

Considering microscopes:

- They have expert and ample references and sources.
- They feel confident and comfortable.
- They are able to work alone for part of the time.
- They have time for thorough investigation.
- They can write analytically.
- They can learn from lecture and reading.
- They can think in abstract terms and language.
- They get a chance to delve into interest areas that are important to them.

Does This Lesson/Unit Build in a Variety of Thinking Skills?

- Is an intelligent behavior included?
- Has successful intelligence been included?
- Have the thinking taxonomies been included?
- Are graphic organizers used to show student thinking?

Also useful is the Checklist of Thinking Activities shown in Figure 5.5.

Figure 5.5   Checklist of Thinking Activities for Teachers Planning Differentiated Learning for Their Students

T	Teacher clarifies and probes for accuracy. Think, Pair, Share increases thinking for all students. Take the thinking to higher levels. Throw out multiple-level questions to multiple students. Take time to probe and question why?
H	Have a series of probes ready. Have a wraparound to keep students engaged and motivated. Have answers supported with proof or evidence. Have language to correct thinking without shutting it down. Have them talk to their classmates, not the teacher.
I	It's important to label the types of thinking that students are using. Include all students: Why do you think? Why do you agree? Disagree? Include process questions, not just facts. Include sufficient "wait time" to let thinking happen without stress. Include students actively with strategies such as "Write, Pair, Share." Involve others in responses: Thumbs up if you agree! Thumbs down if not!
N	Numerous techniques for metacognition should be used. Numerous ways to show acceptance. Interesting!, Never thought about it that way! What else could you add? Why do you believe so? Nod and use body language that is accepting and appreciative. Never interrupt the thinker. Wait 'til they're finished sharing. Probe. Need logs and journals for reflection.
K	Key concepts should be the focus of discussion, thinking, and questions. Kick thinking to all levels of whatever taxonomy you are using. Keep the thinker thinking. TAPS. Compose a rebuttal. Keep encouraging the speaker and the listeners so all dendrites are growing.

Bibliography

Ainsworth, L. (2003a). *Power standards: Identifying the standards that matter the most.* Denver, CO: Advanced Learning Press and Center for Performance Assessment.

Ainsworth, L. (2003b). *Unwrapping the standards: A simple process to make standards manageable.* Denver, CO: Advanced Learning Press and Center for Performance Assessment.

Aronson, E. (1978). *The jigsaw classroom.* Beverly Hills, CA: Sage.

Ausubel, D. P. (1960). The use of advance organizers in the learning and retention of meaningful verbal material. *Journal of Educational Psychology, 51,* 267–272.

Bandler, R., & Grinder, J. (1979). *Frogs into princes.* Moab, UT: Real People Press/Eden Grove Editions.

Barell, J. (2003). *Developing more curious minds.* Alexandria, VA: Association for Supervision and Curriculum Development.

Baron-Cohen, S. (2003). *The essential difference: The truth about the male and female brain.* New York: Basic Books.

Beane, J. (1985–86, December–January). The continuing controversy over affective education. *Educational Leadership,* 26–31.

Bell, L. C. (1986, November). Learning styles in the middle school classroom: Why and how. *Middle School Journal,* 28.

Bellanca, J., & Fogarty, R. (1991). *Blueprints for thinking in the cooperative classroom* (2nd ed.). Arlington Heights, IL: Skylight.

Benton, S. I. (1997). Psychological foundations of elementary writing instruction. In G. D. Phye (Ed.), *Handbook of academic learning: Construction of knowledge* (pp. 235–264). San Diego, CA: Academic Press.

Binet, A., & Simon, T. (1916). *The development of intelligence in children.* Baltimore: Williams & Wilkins. (Reprinted 1973, New York: Arno Press; 1983, Salem, NH: Ayer)

Bloom, B. S. (Ed.). (1956). *Taxonomy of educational objectives handbook 1: Cognitive domain.* New York: Longman, Green.

Blum, D. (1997). *Sex on the brain: The biological differences between men and women.* New York: Viking.

Burns, T. (1996). *From risk to resilience: A journey with heart for our children, our future.* Dallas, TX: Marco Polo Group.

Caine, R., & Caine, G. (1991). *Making connections: Teaching and the human brain.* New York: Addison-Wesley.

Caine, R., & Caine, G. (1997). *Education on the edge of possibility.* Alexandria, VA: Association for Supervision and Curriculum Development.

Caine, R., Caine, G., McClintic, C., & Klimek, K. (2005). *12 brain/mind learning principles in action.* Thousand Oaks, CA: Corwin Press.

Carter, R. (1998). *Mapping the mind.* Los Angeles: University of California Press.

Cawelti, G. (Ed.). (1995). *Handbook of research on improving student achievement.* Arlington, VA: Educational Research Service.

Cherry, C., Godwin, D., & Staples, J. (1989). *Is the left brain always right?* Carthage, IL: Fearon Teacher Aids.

Conner, D. (1993). *Managing at the speed of change.* New York: Villard Books.

Costa, A. (1991). *The school as a home for the mind.* Arlington Heights, IL: Skylight.

Costa, A., & Garmston, R. (1994). *The art of cognitive coaching.* Norwood, MA: Christopher Gordon.

Costa, A., & Garmston, R. (2002). *Cognitive coaching: A foundation for renaissance schools.* Norwood, MA: Christopher Gordon.

Costa, A., & Kallick, B. (2000). *Habits of mind: A developmental series.* Alexandria, VA: Association for Supervision and Curriculum Development.

Covey, S. (1989). *The seven habits of highly effective people.* New York: Simon & Schuster.

Cowan, G., & Cowan, E. (1980). *Writing.* New York: John Wiley.

Csikszentmihalyi, M. (1991). *Flow: The psychology of optimal experience.* New York: Harper Perennial.

Cunningham, D. (1999). *Preschool curriculum: A child centered curriculum of concepts and activities including all of the CDA functional areas.* Washington, DC: ERIC.

Damasio, A. (1994). *Descartes' error: Emotion, reason, and the human brain.* New York: Putnam.

Damasio, A. (1999). *The feeling of what happens: Body and emotion in the making of consciousness.* New York: Harcourt Brace.

Deal, T. E., & Peterson, K. D. (1998). *Shaping school culture: The heart leadership.* San Francisco: Jossey-Bass.

de Bono, E. (1987). *Edward de Bono's CoRT thinking.* Boston: Advanced Practical Thinking.

de Bono, E. (1999). *Six thinking hats.* Boston: Little Brown.

Dennison, P., & Dennison, G. (1989). *Brain gym.* Ventura, CA: Edu-Kinesthetics.

Depree, M. (1989). *Leadership is an art.* New York: Doubleday.

Diamond, M. (1988). *Enriching heredity: The impact of the environment on the autonomy of the brain.* New York: Free Press.

Dunn, K., & Dunn, R. (1987). Dispelling outmoded beliefs about student learning. *Educational Leadership, 44*(6), 55–61.

Dunn, K., & Dunn, R. (1992). *Bringing out the giftedness in your child.* New York: John Wiley.

Dunn, R. (1990). Teaching underachievers through their learning style strengths. *International Education, 16*(52), 5–7.

Eberle, B. (1982). *Scamper: Games for imagination development.* Buffalo, NY: DOK.

Eisner, E. W. (1983). The art and craft of teaching. *Educational Leadership, 40*(4), 4–13.

Fogarty, R., & Bellanca, J. (1993). *Patterns for thinking, patterns for transfer: A cooperative team approach for critical and creative thinking in the classroom.* Arlington Heights, IL: IRI/Skylight.

Fogarty, R., & Stoehr, J. (1995). *Integrating curricula with multiple intelligences: Teams, themes, and threads.* Arlington Heights, IL: IRI/Skylight.

Fraser, B. J., Walberg, H. J., Welch, W. W., & Hattie, J. A. (1987). Synthesis of educational productivity research. *Journal of Educational Research, 11*(2), 145–252.

Gaddy, B. B., Dean, C. B., & Kendall, J. S. (2002). *Noteworthy perspectives: Keeping the focus on learning.* Aurora, CO: Mid-Continent Research for Education and Learning.

Gardner, H. (1985). *Frames of mind: The theory of multiple intelligences.* New York: Basic Books.

Gardner, H. (1993). *Multiple intelligences: The theory in practice.* New York: Basic Books.

Gazzaniga, M. (1998a). *The mind's past.* Berkeley: University of California Press.

Gazzaniga, M. (1998b, July). The split-brain revisited. *Scientific American, 279,* 50–55.

Gibbs, J. (1995). *A new way of learning and being together.* Santa Rosa, CA: Center Source.

Given, B. K. (2002). *The brain's natural learning systems.* Alexandria, VA: Association for Supervision and Curriculum Development.

Goldberg, E. (2001). *The executive brain: Frontal lobes and the civilized mind.* New York: Oxford University Press.

Goleman, D. (1995). *Emotional intelligence.* New York: Bantam.

Goleman, D. (1998). *Working with emotional intelligence.* New York: Bantam.

Gregorc, A. (1982). *Inside styles: Beyond the basics.* Columbia, CT: Gregorc Associates.

Gregory, G. (2003). *Differentiated instructional strategies in practice: Training, implementation, and supervision.* Thousand Oaks, CA: Corwin Press.

Gregory, G., & Chapman, C. (2002). *Differentiating instructional strategies: One size doesn't fit all.* Thousand Oaks, CA: Corwin Press.

Gregory, G., & Kuzmich, L. (2004). *Data driven differentiation in the standards-based classroom.* Thousand Oaks, CA: Corwin Press.

Gregory, G., & Kuzmich, L. (2005a). *Differentiated literacy strategies for student growth and achievement in grades PreK-6.* Thousand Oaks, CA: Corwin Press.

Gregory, G., & Kuzmich, L. (2005b). *Differentiated literacy strategies for student growth and achievement in grades 7–12.* Thousand Oaks, CA: Corwin Press.

Guild, P. B., & Garger, S. (1985). *Marching to different drummers.* Alexandria, VA: Association for Supervision and Curriculum Development.

Gurian, M., Henley, P., & Trueman, T. (2001). *Boys and girls learn differently! A guide for teachers and parents.* San Francisco: Jossey-Bass/John Wiley.

Gurian, M., & Stevens, K. (2004). With boys and girls in mind. *Educational Leadership, 62*(3), 21–26.

Harris, J. R. (1998). *The nature assumption: Why children turn out the way they do.* New York: Free Press.

Hart, L. (2002). *Human brain and human learning* (3rd ed.). Covington, WA: Books for Educators.

Havers, F. (1995). *Rhyming tasks male and female brains differently.* New Haven, CT: Yale University Press.

Healy, J. (1992). *Endangered minds: Why our children don't think.* New York: Simon & Schuster.

Hunter, R. (2004). *Madeline Hunter's master teaching: Increasing instructional effectiveness in elementary and secondary schools.* Thousand Oaks, CA: Corwin Press.

Jacobs, H. H. (1997). *Mapping the big picture: Integrating curriculum and assessment K-12.* Alexandria, VA: Association for Supervision and Curriculum Development.

James, J. (1996). *Thinking in the future tense: A workout for the mind.* New York: Simon & Schuster.

Johnson, D., & Johnson, R. (1991). *Cooperative learning lesson structures*. Edina, MN: Interaction Books.

Johnson, D., & Johnson, R. (1998). *Learning together and alone* (5th ed.). Boston: Allyn & Bacon.

Jung, C. (1923). *Psychological types* (H. G. Baynes, Trans.). New York: Harcourt, Brace.

Kagan, S. (1992). *Cooperative learning*. San Juan Capistrano, CA: Kagan Cooperative Learning.

Kantor, R. M. (1985). Why people resist change. *Management Review*.

Kessler, R. (2000). *The soul of education: Helping students find connection, compassion, and character at school*. Alexandria, VA: Association for Supervision and Curriculum Development.

Kolb, D. (1984). *Experiential learning: Experience as the source of learning and development*. Englewood Cliffs, NJ: Prentice Hall.

Krathwohl, D. R., Bloom, B. S., & Masia, B. B. (1964). *Taxonomy of educational objectives: Handbook II: Affective domain*. New York: David McKay.

Levine, M. (1990). *Keeping ahead in school*. Cambridge, MA: Educator's Publishing Service.

Lowry, D. (1979). *The keys to personal success*. Riverside, CA: True Colors.

Marzano, R. (2003). *What works in schools: Translating research into action*. Alexandria, VA: Association for Supervision and Curriculum Development.

Marzano, R., Norford, J., Paynter, D., Gaddy, B., & Pickering, D. (2001). *Handbook for classroom instruction that works*. Alexandria, VA: Association for Supervision and Curriculum Development.

Marzano, R., Pickering, D., & Pollock, J. (2001). *Classroom instruction that works: Research-based strategies for increasing student achievement*. Alexandria, VA: Association for Supervision and Curriculum Development.

McCarthy, B. (1990). Using the 4MAT system to bring learning styles to schools. *Education Leadership, 48*(2), 31–33.

McCarthy, B. (2000). *About teaching: 4MAT in the classroom*. Wanconda, FL: About Learning.

McCombs, B., & Whistler, S. (1997). *The learner-centered classroom and school: Strategies for increasing student motivation and achievement*. San Francisco: Jossey-Bass.

McNeeley, C., Nonnemaker, J., & Blum, R. (2002). Promoting school connectedness: Evidence from the National Longitudinal Study of Adolescent Health. *Journal of School Health, 72*(40), 138–146.

McTighe, J., & Lyman, F. (1988). Cueing thinking in the classroom: The promise of theory-embedded tools. *Educational Leadership, 45*(7), 18–24.

Milgram, R., Dunn, R., & Price, G. (1993). *Teaching and counseling gifted and talented adolescents*. Westport, CT: Praeger.

Moir, A., & Jessel, D. (1989). *Brain sex: The real difference between men and women*. New York: Dell.

Nagy, W. (2000). *Teaching vocabulary to improve reading comprehension*. Washington, DC: NCTE and ERIC.

Naisbitt, J. (1982). *Megatrends: Ten new directions transforming our lives*. New York: Warner Books.

November, A. (2001). *Empowering students with technology*. Arlington Heights, IL: Skylight.

O'Keefe, J., & Nadel, L. (1978). *The hippocampus as a cognitive map*. Oxford, UK: Clarendon Press.

Orlich, D., Harder, R., Callahan, R., Kravas, C., Kauchak, D., Pendergrass, R. A., Keogh, A., & Hellene, D. (1980). *Teaching strategies: A guide to better instruction*. Lexington, MA: D. C. Heath.

Ornstein, R. (1986). *Multimind: A new way of looking at human behavior*. New York: Doubleday.

Ornstein, R., & Sobel, D. (1987). *The healing brain*. New York: Simon & Schuster.

Palmer, P. (1993). *To know as we are known*. San Francisco: Harper San Francisco.

Panksepp, J. (1998). *Affective neuroscience: The foundations of human and animal emotions*. New York: Oxford University Press.

Parry, T., & Gregory, G. (2003). *Designing brain compatible learning*. Arlington Heights, IL: Skylight.

Paul, R., & Elder, L. (2001). *Critical thinking tools for taking charge of your learning and your life*. New Jersey: Prentice Hall.

Perkins, D. (1995). *Outsmarting IQ*. New York: Free Press.

Pert, C. (1993). The chemical communicators. In B. Moyers (Ed.), *Healing and the mind*. New York: Doubleday.

Peters, T. J., & Austin, N. (1985). *A passion for excellence: The leadership difference*. New York: Warner Books.

Purdom, D. M. (1984). *A simple guide to using Bloom's taxonomy*. Tampa: University of South Florida.

Quellmalz, E. S. (1985). Developing reasoning skills. In J. R. Baron & R. J. Sternberg (Eds.), *Teaching thinking skills: Theory and practice* (pp. 86–105). New York: Freeman.

Reeves, D. B. (2000). *Accountability in action: A blueprint for learning organizations*. Denver, CO: Advanced Learning Press and Center for Performance Assessment.

Reeves, D. B. (2003). *The daily disciplines of leadership*. Denver, CO: Advanced Learning Press and Center for Performance Assessment.

Restak, R. (1994). *The modular brain*. New York: Vintage.

Rich, B. (Ed.). (2000). *The Dana brain daybook*. New York: Charles A. Dana Foundation.

Rickard, P., & Stiles, R. (1985). Comprehensive adult student assessment system design for effective assessment in correctional educational programs. *Journal of Correctional Education, 36*(2), 51–53.

Roeber, E. (1996). *Guidelines for the development and management of performance assessments* (ERIC Digest No. 410229). Washington, DC: ERIC Clearinghouse on Assessment and Evaluation.

Rowe, M. B. (1986). Wait time: Slowing down may be a way of speeding up. *Education, 11*(1), 43.

Rozman, D. (1998). Speech at Symposium on the Brain, University of California, Berkeley, March.

Salovey, P., & Mayer, J. D. (1990). Emotional intelligence. *Imagination, Cognition, and Personality, 9*, 185–211.

Salovey, P., & Sluyter, D. J. (1997). *Emotional development and emotional intelligence: Educational implications*. New York: Basic Books.

Sapolsky, R. M. (1998). *Why zebras don't get ulcers*. New York: W. H. Freeman.

Silver, H. F., & Hanson, J. R. (1998). *Learning styles and strategies* (3rd ed.). Woodbridge, NJ: The Thoughtful Education Press.

Silver, H. F., Strong, R. W., & Perini, M. J. (2001). *Learning style/multiple intelligences checklist*. Woodbridge, NJ: Thoughtful Education Press.

Smilkstein, R. (2003). *We're born to learn: Using the brain's natural learning process to create today's curriculum*. Thousand Oaks, CA: Corwin Press.

Sousa, D. (2001). *How the brain learns* (2nd ed.). Thousand Oaks, CA: Corwin Press.

Sperry, R. (1968). Hemisphere connection and unity consciousness awareness. *American Psychologist, 23,* 723–733.

Sternberg, R. (1996). *Successful intelligence*. New York: Simon & Schuster.

Stiggins, R. J. (1997). *Student-centered classroom assessment* (2nd ed.). Columbus, OH: Merrill.

Stigler, J. W., & Hiebert, J. (1999). *The teaching gap: Best ideas from the world's teachers for improving education in the classroom*. New York: Free Press.

Swartz, R. J., & Perkins, D. (1990). *Teaching thinking: Issues and approaches*. Pacific Grove, CA: Critical Press and Thinking Software.

Sylwester, R. (1995). *A celebration of neurons: An educator's guide to the brain*. Alexandria, VA: Association for Supervision and Curriculum Development.

Sylwester, R. (2005). *How to explain a brain: An educator's handbook of brain terms and cognitive processes*. Thousand Oaks, CA: Corwin Press.

Taylor, S. (2002). *The tending instinct*. New York: Times Books.

Thornburg, D. (2002). *The new basics education and the future of work in the telematic age*. Alexandria, VA: Association for Supervision and Curriculum Development.

Tomlinson, C. (2001). *How to differentiate instruction in mixed-ability classrooms* (2nd ed.). Alexandria, VA: Association for Supervision and Curriculum Development.

U.S. Secretary of Labor. (1991). *What work requires of schools: A SCANS report for America 2000*. The Secretary's Commission on Achieving Necessary Skills (SCANS). Washington, DC: Author.

Vail, P. (1989). *Smart kids with school problems*. New York: New American Library.

Walsh, J. A., & Sattes, B. D. (2005). *Quality questioning: Research-based practice to engage every learner*. Thousand Oaks, CA: Corwin Press.

Wasley, P., Hampel, R., & Clark, R. (1997). *Kids and school reform*. San Francisco: Jossey-Bass.

Wiggins, G., & McTighe, J. (1998). *Understanding by design*. Alexandria, VA: Association for Supervision and Curriculum Development.

Williams, F. (1970). *Classroom ideas for encouraging thinking and feeling*. Buffalo, NY: DOK.

Williams, F. (1972). *A total creativity program for individualizing and humanizing the learning process*. Englewood Cliffs, NJ: Educational Technology Publications.

Williams, F. (1989). Creativity assessment packet. In S. L. Schurr (Ed.), *Dynamite in the classroom: A how-to handbook for teachers*. Columbus, OH: Nation Middle School Association.

Williams, F. (1993). The cognitive-affective interaction model for enriching gifted programs. In J. S. Renzulli (Ed.), *Systems and models for developing programs for the gifted and talented* (pp. 461–484). Highett, Victoria, Australia: Hawker Brownlow Education.

Williams, J., & Ryan, J. (2000). National testing and the improvement of classroom teaching: Can they coexist? *British Educational Research Journal, 26*(1), 49–74.

Witelson, S. (2004, May). *The male and female brain: The same but different* [Speech]. Hamilton, Ontario, Canada.

Wolfe, P. (2001). *Brain matters: Translating research into classroom practice.* Alexandria, VA: Association for Supervision and Curriculum Development.

Wright, R. (1994). *The moral animal.* New York: Vintage.

Index

Note: Page numbers marked with an *f* are figures.

**CORWIN
PRESS**

The Corwin Press logo—a raven striding across an open book—represents the union of courage and learning. Corwin Press is committed to improving education for all learners by publishing books and other professional development resources for those serving the field of K–12 education. By providing practical, hands-on materials, Corwin Press continues to carry out the promise of its motto: **"Helping Educators Do Their Work Better."**